SALESQUALIFYD

FOR STARTUPS TO LAUNCH IN THREE WEEKS!

BALAJI VIJAYARAGHAVAN

To those young geeks aspiring to emerge a unicorn, persistently!

Importantly to 20 of the CEOs (deliberately not naming them as I'm bound by NDAs with some) who trusted me to launch their product, as of Aug'2023, the launch of this book, I have had the opportunity of launching 44 SaaS products, touchwood, all are doing well in the market!

Contents

Contents

Preface

In 2011, my journey as a freelance writer began, and I found myself covering events and conferences for small media outlets in the vibrant city of Chennai. However, during those early days, my language skills were abysmal. Little did I know that my passion for cricket, which I had secretly followed on the radio in classrooms, would play a crucial role in transforming my abilities. As I closely visualized the shots executed by batsmen and the fielding acrobatics of the players, my vocabulary and articulation began to take shape.

In this quest for improvement, I found a remarkable source of inspiration in the voice of cricket - none other than Harsha Bhogle. His eloquence and profound analysis of the game became my beacon, driving me to become a wordsmith with the intent to immerse readers in the scene, making them feel a part of the action.

Over the years, my reputation for writing and speaking prowess grew, and I became the go-to person for my classmates, helping them craft everything from leave letters to heartwarming love letters. As my skills expanded, so did my career, and between 2011 and 2016, I ventured into the realms of advertising and digital marketing.

Then, in mid-2017, a significant shift awaited me as I stepped into the dynamic world of B2B SaaS. It was a leap into uncharted territory, where I found myself working with startups in the EdTech, Healthcare, and Energy & Power sectors. The process of launching products proved to be an emotional roller coaster, demanding late-night stays in the office and presenting challenges to overcome.

Amidst the frenzy, two profound moments of inspiration guided me towards transformative insights. Harsha Bhogle's TED talk about the unique pace of work in India resonated with me, while my mentor, the former Director General of Police, Dr. Prateep Philip, often shared about the potential for personal change within a three-week window.

Combining these ideas, I devised the Three Week Theory, a carefully crafted checklist manifesto to maintain work-life balance and preserve mental well-being during intense product launches. It became an internal compass, ensuring that no stone was left unturned as we prepared to Go To Market.

As my journey evolved, I took on the role of a management consulting professional, aligning myself with the world of sales while retaining my focus on marketing strategies. My confidence in persuasive writing, with a 100% success rate in crafting compelling love letters for friends, provided the validation I needed.

The Three Week Theory matured over time, and I introduced Salesqualifyd as a valuable offering to the founders I consulted. Now, after years of refining and fine-tuning my approach, I present this book as a comprehensive guide to help you navigate the intricate path of preparing your B2B SaaS platform for a seamless Go To Market journey. With 21 chapters, encompassing one activity for each day for three weeks, you can choose to give a run-through of each topic in depth, reviewing more resources.

Between 2016 and the present day, I have had the privilege of assisting over 20 founders and successfully launching 44 products. Each endeavor has been met with favorable outcomes, and it fills me with a sense of gratitude.

The journey from identifying the Ideal Customer Profile, product validation, to achieving the coveted product-market fit, is all covered to perfection.

Throughout this adventure, I have held this creation close to my heart, cherishing it as mine. However, today marks a pivotal moment as I pass the torch to you, dear reader. Henceforth, this book becomes yours, champion! It is my sincerest hope that the experiences, and insights within these pages will empower you to make a lasting impact and drive your B2B SaaS platform to unparalleled success.

Foreword

I am delighted to write this foreword, and during one of the startup events, I had the pleasure of meeting Balaji. Upon approaching him, he agreed to guide us in defining our GTM (Go-to-Market) strategy with a hard-pressed deadline of 4 weeks. Remarkably, he developed a 3-week checklist that worked wonders for us. Since then, Balaji has been working closely with us in our operations.

I must admit that despite my 15 years of experience as a marketing communication specialist, I had overlooked and underestimated certain obvious steps in GTM, and at times, I had overengineered certain aspects. Balaji's outlook offers a well-balanced approach, and this book provides invaluable guidance in that regard.

Upon perusing this magnificent book, I am absolutely amazed by Balaji's talent and dedication in sharing his experiences of launching various SaaS products over the years. The book is a goldmine of information, presented in simple steps and techniques, covering even the minutest details. It will undoubtedly serve as a highly informative and handy reference for those in the early stages of a startup. In short, Balaji's Book is unique and truly a treasure trove for anyone working on an idea, Product-Market fit, and Go-to-Market strategies, making it a must-read for all founders.

Arun CR
Founder & CEO
Realiti.io

ONE

Embracing the Power of Intent

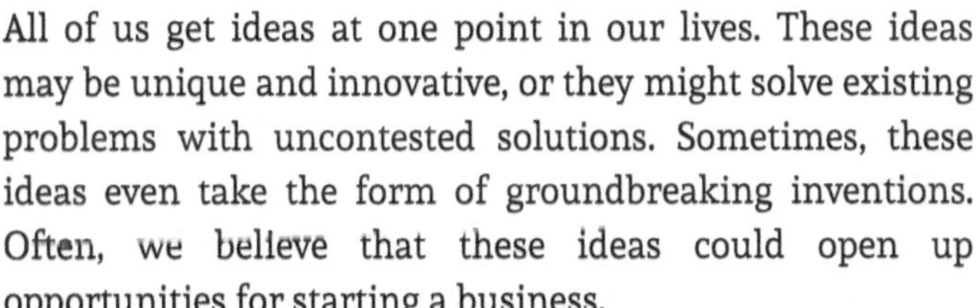

All of us get ideas at one point in our lives. These ideas may be unique and innovative, or they might solve existing problems with uncontested solutions. Sometimes, these ideas even take the form of groundbreaking inventions. Often, we believe that these ideas could open up opportunities for starting a business.

However, amid the excitement, one formidable obstacle stands in our way: self-doubt. The questions start to crowd our minds: Will it work? Am I cut out for entrepreneurship? Where do I even begin? How can I secure funding? How do I find my target customers? Will my business offerings be valued? Can I generate revenue? Will I ever achieve profitability?

In the face of these doubts, let us contemplate the words of Simon Sinek, "People don't buy for what you do. They buy for why you do it." This profound statement encapsulates the essence of entrepreneurial success: understanding your intent.

Finding Purpose Through Inspiration:

Consider the story of Girish Mathrubootham, the visionary founder of Freshdesk (now a part of Freshworks). A life-altering incident during his flight from the USA to India, where his LCD TV broke, exposed the flaws in customer support systems. This experience, fraught with frustration, made him realize the dire need for a customer-centric approach in the industry. As a tech-savvy individual, Girish saw the opportunity to bridge this gap using a robust SaaS platform. Freshworks, under his leadership, evolved into a revolutionary force that redefined the very fabric of customer support.

The story of Girish serves as a beacon of inspiration, but not every intent needs to be born out of such significant events. It can be as simple as a wish, a daydream, or a desire to create something remarkable. Whatever the source, understanding the 'why' behind your entrepreneurial journey is fundamental to success.

The Power of Intent:

Identifying your intent can be a transformative process. It is more than just defining your business concept; it is about unraveling the essence of your vision, values, and long-term goals. Your intent should resonate with your deepest beliefs and passions. When your intent is clear, it serves as the driving force behind every decision you make and every action you take.

Purposeful Reflection:

To unveil your intent, take the time for introspection. Reflect on what truly motivates you and what you wish to achieve with your entrepreneurial endeavor. Ask yourself why you are drawn to this particular idea and how it aligns with your personal values. Consider the impact you envision creating in the world and how your business can make a meaningful difference.

Articulate Your Mission:

Once you have clarity on your intent, articulate it into a compelling mission statement. This concise declaration should encapsulate your purpose, target audience, and the transformative impact you aim to create.

Remember, a well-defined mission statement not only guides you but also attracts like-minded individuals to join your journey.

For example, let's imagine you are passionate about sustainable fashion and wish to create an eco-friendly clothing brand that empowers local artisans. Your mission statement could be: "Our mission is to revolutionize the fashion industry by producing sustainable, ethically-made clothing that celebrates local craftsmanship, protects the environment, and empowers communities."

Assemble Your Tribe:

Building a team that shares your vision is pivotal. Talent can be found for specific job descriptions, but it takes more to create a cohesive and aligned team.

Seek individuals who resonate with your intent and are passionate about contributing to your shared mission.

Look for individuals with not only the right skills but also the right mindset, as a team that believes in the 'why' behind your business is more likely to stay committed during challenging times.

Consider incorporating a hiring process that assesses candidates' alignment with your mission and values.

Conduct interviews that delve into their personal aspirations and gauge their passion for the greater purpose your business aims to serve.

Nurture a Purposeful Culture:

A strong intent fuels a vibrant company culture. Foster an environment that encourages innovation, open communication, and a shared commitment to the greater purpose. When your team is connected with your 'why,' they become inspired contributors, propelling your business towards success.

Promote transparency and communication within your team. Regularly share your mission and progress, allowing everyone to understand their roles in the collective journey. Encourage collaboration and the sharing of ideas, as diverse perspectives can lead to innovative solutions aligned with your intent.

Embrace Adversity:

The entrepreneurial journey is not without challenges. However, when your intent is unwavering, adversities become stepping stones instead of roadblocks. Embrace challenges as opportunities to refine your intent and grow stronger as a team.

Stay true to your mission during difficult times. Seek feedback from your customers and team members to continually improve and align your offerings with your intent. Embrace failures as valuable learning experiences that bring you closer to fulfilling your purpose.

Communicate Your Intent:

Your intent is not only for internal consumption; it should also resonate with your customers. Authenticity and transparency are essential in building trust and loyalty with your audience. Clearly communicate your 'why' through your branding, marketing, and customer interactions.

Tell the story of how your business began and the driving force behind it. Show your customers the positive impact they are contributing to by supporting your business. Invite them to join your journey and become a part of something larger than themselves.

In conclusion, the power of intent can transform your entrepreneurial journey from a vague idea to a purpose-driven mission. Embrace your why and let it guide you through the uncertain terrains of entrepreneurship. Girish Mathrubootham's experience with Freshworks exemplifies the potential of intent, a potent force that reshapes industries and touches lives.

As you embark on your path, remember that intent is not merely a concept but a living, breathing force that fuels your vision. It is your guiding star and the heart of your entrepreneurial spirit. Let it light your way and attract like-minded souls who share your passion and drive.

The world awaits your purposeful intent. Embrace it, nurture it, and set forth to create an impact that reverberates far beyond your wildest dreams.

The journey of intent-driven entrepreneurship is an evolving one, and with every step you take, you bring your vision closer to reality. Embrace the power of intent, and let it become the driving force that propels you to success and fulfillment.

TWO

PERSONALIZING YOUR APPROACH: UNDERSTANDING YOUR TARGET GROUP

In the competitive business landscape, understanding your target group is more than just broad classifications. It involves recognizing the intricacies of your customers' needs, interests, and personalities.

To stand out in the market, you must answer the compelling "why" that motivates customers to choose your business—a Unique Selling Point (USP).

But the question remains: for whom should your USP be unique? This chapter aims to help you navigate this challenge, ensuring your USP resonates with customers and adds value from their perspective.

There is no one-size-fits-all:

Every customer is a unique individual, with their own preferences and personality traits. While you may categorize them into segments based on demographics, lifestyle, industry, and more, it's essential to view them as humans with distinct personalities.

Understanding their uniqueness empowers you to pitch your offerings "FOR" your customers, addressing their specific needs and interests.

Business-to-Consumer (B2C) and Business-to-Business (B2B) Offerings:

Whether your target group consists of individual consumers or a group of decision-makers within a business, remember that it is ultimately a human being who becomes your point of contact. Irrespective of the B2C or B2B nature, personalization remains key to connecting with your customers effectively.

Pitching "FOR" Your Customers:

To engage your customers authentically, shift your focus from pitching "TO" them to pitching "FOR" them. This shift in perspective requires a deeper understanding of not only their needs but also their character, personality, and interests.

Empathy and genuine concern for your customers will make your business offering more valuable to them.

Develop User Personas:

As your customer base grows, maintaining personalization can be challenging. To address this, create user personas—fictional characters representing your ideal customers.

These personas serve as a reference for crafting personalized marketing strategies and nurturing meaningful connections.

Step 1: Define Target Sectors:

Begin by identifying the sectors you plan to cater to and classify them into industries and sub-segments. For example, if your business is in the energy and power sector, segment it into solar, wind, electric, gas, and hydropower industries, each with its unique requirements.

Step 2: Analyze Demographics & Region:

Personalization is the key to effectively connect with your customers. Consider regional nuances and preferences when defining the geographic regions you want to target. Tailoring your offerings to specific locations enhances customer satisfaction.

Step 3: Understand Professional Identity:

Determine the range of job titles you wish to engage with, from top-level executives to entry-level employees. This knowledge will enable you to communicate effectively and address your customers' specific needs.

Step 4: Explore Personal Interests:

While not the primary focus, understanding your customers' personal interests can help you create meaningful connections. Factors such as music preferences, sports affiliations, and hobbies provide valuable insights for tailored interactions.

Step 5: Respect Cultural Identity:

Respecting cultural sensitivities ensures your communications align with your customers' beliefs and values. Avoid sharing information that may contradict their cultural norms, fostering a sense of respect and understanding.

A Quick Activity:

Identify three potential customers with varied job titles, sectors, and specializations. This exercise will aid in brand positioning, setting up nurture streams, and crafting personalized content. Fill in the details for each individual, as outlined below:

First Name:

Last Name:

Job Title:

Company Name:

Company Sector:

Specialization:

City:

Country:

Preferred Language:

Personal Interests:

Understanding your target group as unique individuals is the foundation of personalized marketing and meaningful connections. By pitching "FOR" your customers and creating user personas, you can offer solutions that align with their specific needs and interests. As you expand your business and reach out to more customers, remember the power of personalization.

THREE

Identifying Your Competitors: Navigating the Blue Ocean

In the fiercely competitive SaaS B2B software industry, identifying your competitors goes beyond mere curiosity; it's about discovering the untapped opportunities that set your business apart. Embracing the Blue Ocean Strategy, we steer away from conventional head-to-head competition (Red Ocean) and set our sights on uncontested market spaces.

This chapter delves into the art of identifying competitors and leveraging the Blue Ocean approach, empowering you to make your competition irrelevant and forge a path to success.

Understanding the Blue Ocean Strategy:

The Blue Ocean Strategy, conceptualized by W. Chan Kim and Renée Mauborgne, revolves around uncovering unexplored market spaces where competition is minimal or non-existent. Unlike the Red Ocean, where businesses fiercely compete for a limited market share, the Blue Ocean offers boundless opportunities for innovation and growth. By charting your course in the Blue Ocean, you create new demand and make your competition irrelevant.

Step 1: Find the Key Business Offering Keyword:

To identify your competitors, conduct an in-depth keyword search related to your core SaaS B2B software offering. For instance, if you provide project management solutions, conduct a search for "project management software for businesses." This search will yield a list of prominent players in the market, laying the foundation for further analysis.

Case Study: Exploring the Project Management Software Industry

Suppose your SaaS B2B software company offers a comprehensive project management solution for businesses of all sizes. Conducting a keyword search for "project management software for businesses" reveals several key players dominating the market. List them in a spreadsheet to proceed with the evaluation.

Step 2: Analyze Competitor Features and Usability:

Next, delve into the features and functionalities of each competitor's software. List their top five features in separate columns, highlighting what is offered for free (in amber) and what comes with a cost (in green). Additionally, evaluate the usability of their platforms by rating their user experience on a scale of 10. This comprehensive analysis provides valuable insights into how different players deliver their solutions to customers.

Case Study: Evaluating Project Management Software Competitors

For project management software, features may include task tracking, collaboration tools, reporting capabilities, and integrations with other apps. By comparing competitors' features and usability, you can identify areas where they excel and areas where they may fall short.

Step 3: Adopt the Customer's Perspective:

Step into the shoes of your potential customers and identify the one aspect that's missing or could be improved in each competitor's software. It may be related to pricing plans, specific project management features, or integration options. To gather this valuable information, review customer feedback, explore industry forums, and study case studies.

Case Study: Addressing Unmet Customer Needs in Project Management Software

Customer feedback reveals that existing project management software lacks seamless integration with other essential tools used by businesses. By addressing this gap and offering seamless integrations, your software can position itself strategically as a unique and valuable solution in the market.

Step 4: Classify Pricing Plans:

Categorize your competitors' pricing plans into Free, Basic, Mid, and Premium segments. Evaluate what features are included in each tier and compare their pricing structures. This analysis enables you to identify potential areas for differentiation in your own pricing strategy.

Case Study: Strategizing Pricing Plans for Project Management Software

Competitors in the project management software realm may offer free plans with limited features, basic plans with essential functionalities, mid-tier plans with advanced features, and premium plans with comprehensive solutions and priority support.

Step 5: Analyze Revenue and Growth:

Gaining insights into your competitors' revenue and growth trajectories provides a better understanding of their market position and overall success. Utilize tools like Owler or InstaFinancials to access relevant data. Analyzing this information helps you make informed decisions about your business's growth strategy.

Understanding competitors' revenue growth can guide your own growth plans, whether you focus on gradual expansion or seek funding to scale more rapidly.

Identifying competitors in the SaaS B2B software industry is an art that requires a thorough analysis of their features, pricing plans, and growth trends. By adopting the Blue Ocean Strategy and focusing on addressing unmet customer needs, you can position your software as a unique and indispensable solution in the market.

Embrace innovation, and let the Blue Ocean guide you to new horizons of growth and competitiveness, where the competition becomes a distant memory, and your business flourishes in uncharted waters.

FOUR

BRAND POSITIONING: UNLEASHING THE ESSENCE OF YOUR BUSINESS IDENTITY

Brand positioning is the art of shaping how your business is perceived by consumers, resonating with their needs, challenges, and aspirations. It goes beyond mere marketing jargon; it is the essence of your business identity and what sets you apart from the competition. In this chapter, we will explore the three essential steps to create a compelling brand positioning strategy that enhances credibility with your target audience and propels your business into the Blue Ocean of uncontested market space.

Step 1: Understanding Your Consumers through Competitor Analysis:

The journey towards effective brand positioning begins with a comprehensive competitor analysis, as discussed in the previous chapter. By studying your competitors' value propositions and analyzing why customers choose them, you gain valuable insights into what your consumers are looking for. For B2C products, understanding customer preferences may be challenging, but for B2B products, there is usually a well-documented study. Though you may not get direct answers, strategic assumptions and assessments will aid in identifying consumer needs.

Case Study: Insights from Project Management Software Competitor Analysis

For our case study in the project management software industry, competitor analysis revealed that customers seek seamless integration with other essential tools. They prioritize user-friendly interfaces, customizable features, and value-for-money pricing plans.

Step 2: Crafting Your Unique Selling Proposition (USP):

To create an impactful brand positioning, focus on how you can differentiate your business offering. Packaging your product differently doesn't necessarily mean altering the core solution; it can encompass innovative delivery methods, unique features based on pricing plans, and a strong USP. Developing a compelling USP opens doors to uncontested market spaces, leading your business towards the Blue Ocean.

Case Study: Project Management Software USP - Seamless Integration & Customization

Building on our case study, our software's USP could be "Seamless Integration & Customization: Tailored Solutions for Enhanced Efficiency." By addressing the unmet need for integration and customization, we position our brand in an untapped market space.

Step 3: Reflecting Your Brand Personality Across All Touchpoints:

Your brand should carry a distinct personality that resonates with your target audience. This personality should reflect consistently across all branding exercises, including your communications, design elements, and products/services. To breathe life into your brand, follow these steps:

Define Your Brand Personality:

Treat your brand as a living entity with its own personality. Define your team's collective entity, envisioning the emotions and values you wish to evoke in your customers.

Naming Your Brand:

Choose a name that aligns with your brand personality and resonates with your target audience. Ensure it is relevant to your industry and complements your brand's essence.

Identify Brand Colors:

Select colors that embody your brand personality and archetype. Determine how you want your brand to be perceived - whether as trustworthy, dependable, warm, or bold.

Logo Design & Colors:

Evaluate your existing logo design and colors against your brand personality and archetype. If necessary, redesign to ensure consistency and resonance with your brand identity.

Case Study: Embodying Brand Personality in Project Management Software

Our project management software brand, named "EfficientFlow," aims to reflect trust, clarity, and dependability through a seamless and customizable user experience. The logo design incorporates simple yet professional elements, while blue and green colors evoke a sense of efficiency and harmony.

Brand positioning is a powerful tool that allows you to carve a unique identity in the market and resonate with your target consumers. By understanding consumer needs through competitor analysis, crafting a compelling USP, and consistently reflecting your brand personality, you can unleash the essence of your business identity and drive towards uncontested market spaces.

Remember, successful brand positioning requires dedication, consistency, and a deep understanding of your target audience. As you position your brand strategically, embrace the Blue Ocean approach, and let it guide you to success in the ever-evolving landscape of the SaaS B2B software industry. Your brand's distinct personality will foster connections with consumers, making it a beacon of trust and reliability in the market. So, embark on this journey with passion and purpose, and let your brand shine brightly in the Blue Ocean of opportunities.

FIVE

Open Up Private Beta - Getting Feedback for Refinement and Success

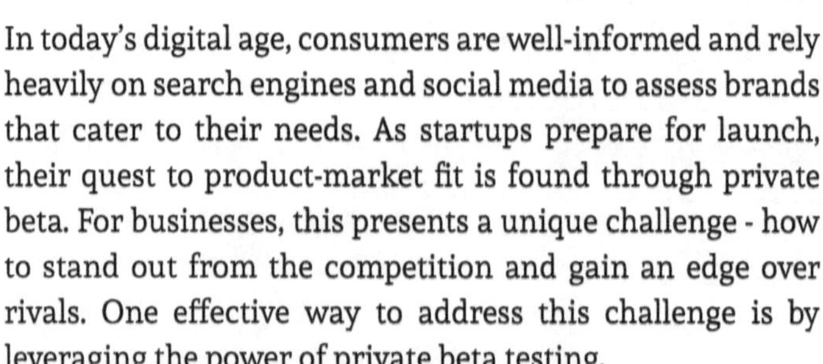

In today's digital age, consumers are well-informed and rely heavily on search engines and social media to assess brands that cater to their needs. As startups prepare for launch, their quest to product-market fit is found through private beta. For businesses, this presents a unique challenge - how to stand out from the competition and gain an edge over rivals. One effective way to address this challenge is by leveraging the power of private beta testing.

In this chapter, we will delve into the concept of private beta, its benefits, and a step-by-step guide on how to execute a successful private beta program.

The Power of Private Beta Testing:

Private beta testing is a targeted approach where select users, often drawn from closed networks and relevant forums, are invited to experience and provide feedback on a business offering before its public release.

Unlike public beta testing, private beta is not about generating revenue; instead, it focuses on gaining valuable insights to refine the product or service.

1.1 Leveraging Private Beta for Advantage:

By offering a private beta to potential customers, businesses can identify unique needs and requirements that competitors might overlook.

It allows them to fine-tune their offerings and create a strong value proposition that resonates with the target audience.

1.2 Building Trust and Credibility:

Private beta participants feel valued and involved in the development process.

This fosters a sense of trust and credibility with the brand, as users understand that their feedback is genuinely valued and can influence the final product.

Identifying Private Beta Users:

2.1 Leveraging Existing Networks:

Leverage your existing network of contacts and relevant forums where you can find potential customers for your business offering.

Startup-related forums and specialized groups are ideal for finding users who align with your target audience.

2.2 Telling an Impactful Story:

Introduce your brand and its purpose with an impactful and genuine story.

This personalized approach resonates better with potential users and helps establish a genuine connection.

Embracing Feedback:

3.1 Focus on Collaboration, Not Selling:

During the private beta, avoid hard selling. Instead, seek help and ask users for critical feedback. Engage in one-on-one sessions with users to gather valuable insights and understand their needs better.

3.2 Activate a Mailing List:

Create a mailing list and segment users based on their industry, job title, and location. Share relevant information with them that aligns with their needs, while also serving your own purpose.

Setting Up the Private Beta:

4.1 Determine the Number of Users:

For enterprise solutions, limit private beta to around five users for in-depth feedback. B2B products can accommodate up to 100 users, and B2C services through technology can have up to 1000 users. Remember, quality feedback is crucial.

4.2 Documenting the Process:

Create comprehensive documentation, including step-by-step guides and research notes about your user's brand requirements. Addressing basic questions beforehand will streamline the testing process.

4.3 Customer Support System:

Establish a robust customer support system using tools like Freshdesk, Zohodesk, or Zendesk to handle support queries promptly and efficiently.

4.4 Enable Feature Requests:

Invite users to submit feature requests based on their needs and challenges. This helps identify unique requirements that may not have been considered earlier.

Rolling out a private beta is a strategic move that helps businesses gain a competitive edge by refining their offerings based on real user feedback. By engaging potential customers in the development process, businesses build trust and credibility, fostering a sense of ownership and loyalty among users. The power of private beta lies not only in fine-tuning your business offering but also in creating an emotional connection with your target audience. So, embrace the private beta process, leverage user feedback, and position your brand for success in the competitive market landscape. Remember, the insights gained from private beta testing will propel your business towards uncontested market spaces, solidifying your position as a leader in your industry.

SIX

Mastering the Art of Pitch Deck Preparation

Preparing a compelling pitch deck is an essential skill for every business professional, whether you're presenting to potential clients, partners, investors, mentors, or regulators.

A well-crafted pitch deck has the power to captivate your audience, convey your value proposition effectively, and pave the way for successful interactions.

In this chapter, we will explore the key elements of a pitch deck and provide a step-by-step guide to help you create impressive presentations that leave a lasting impact.

The Purpose of a Pitch Deck:

A pitch deck serves as a supporting document for your pitch and should never overshadow the presenter. It must strike a balance between being comprehensive when shared with stakeholders and being crisp when presented live to an audience. The purpose of a pitch deck is to engage, inform, and persuade your audience while aligning with your brand aesthetics.

Slide-by-Slide Guide:

Slide 1: Introduction

Start your pitch deck with a visually appealing slide that includes your logo and a creative element representing your business offering. This slide should leave a positive first impression and set the tone for the rest of the presentation.

Slide 2: Brief about the Presenter(s)

Introduce the key presenters with a brief description of their background, expertise, and role within the organization. Establishing credibility early on helps build trust with your audience.

Slide 3: Agenda/Index

Outline the contents of your pitch deck in a clear and concise manner. A well-structured agenda allows your audience to follow the flow of the presentation and know what to expect.

Slide 4: About the Organization

Provide an overview of your organization, including its inception, industry, and core expertise. Use this slide to establish your brand's identity and showcase your understanding of the market.

Slide 5: Market Gap and Challenges Addressed

Identify the existing market gap or challenges your business offering seeks to address. Present data, statistics, or real-life examples to highlight the problem you aim to solve.

Slide 6: Solutions Offered and Value Proposition

Present your solutions and clearly outline your value proposition. Showcase how your business offering stands out from the competition and meets the needs of your target audience.

Slide 7: Key Features, Capabilities & USP

Elaborate on the key features, capabilities, and unique selling proposition (USP) of your product or service. Use this slide to emphasize the benefits customers will gain by choosing your offering.

Slide 8: Competitors - Direct & Indirect

Identify your direct and indirect competitors and provide a brief comparison of your strengths and advantages. Show how your business offering differentiates itself from competitors.

Slide 9: Market Share, Strategy, and Target Groups

Share your market share, strategies for growth, and target customer segments. Showcase your understanding of the market dynamics and how you plan to capture your desired audience.

Slide 10: Infrastructures and Technologies Used

Detail the infrastructures and technologies employed to deliver your product or service. Highlight any cutting-edge technologies or unique approaches that give you a competitive edge.

Slide 11: Product or Organization Roadmap

Outline the future roadmap for your product or organization. Share your vision for growth and any upcoming developments that will enhance your offering.

Slide 12: Financial Projections

Present financial projections, including revenue forecasts, expenses, and profitability estimates. Transparency and realistic projections build confidence among potential investors.

Slide 13: Usage & Documentation

Explain how customers can use your product or service and provide documentation to support their journey. Make it easy for them to understand and navigate your offering.

Slide 14: Customer Support & Requests

Emphasize the importance of customer support and showcase the mechanisms in place to handle queries and requests. Demonstrating your commitment to customer satisfaction is crucial.

Slide 15: Contact & Thank You

End your pitch deck with clear contact information for the audience to reach out. Express gratitude and thank your audience for their time and attention.

Personalization and Branding:

Remember, each pitch deck should be tailored to the specific audience you're presenting to. Personalize the content to resonate with their needs, challenges, and interests. Additionally, ensure that the slide designs, colors, and language align with your brand aesthetics.

Mastery through Practice:

Preparing pitch decks is an ongoing process of learning and improvement. The more you practice, the better you will become at creating engaging and persuasive presentations.

Utilize the vast collection of slide templates provided with this book and explore online resources to refine your pitch deck skills.

Mastering the art of pitch deck preparation is a fundamental skill for any business professional. A well-crafted pitch deck can significantly impact your success in engaging potential clients, investors, and partners.

By following the slide-by-slide guide and personalizing your pitch decks, you can create compelling presentations that captivate your audience, convey your value proposition effectively, and ultimately lead to successful outcomes for your business. So, unleash your creativity, embrace the power of persuasion, and prepare to pitch for the win!

SEVEN

BETA LAUNCH PLATFORMS - PULSE OF THE STARTUP ECOSYSTEM

In today's inclusive startup ecosystem, tech startups have a plethora of platforms available to showcase their products and connect with potential users. These platforms go beyond simple listings; they act as magazines, forums, and social networks that bring together innovators, early adopters, and the critical mass needed for a successful go-to-market strategy.

In this chapter, we will explore the significance of beta launch platforms and provide a comprehensive list of 206 such sites to help you kickstart your startup's journey. Write to me to get that complete list of beta launch sites.

The Power of Early Adopters:

In the innovation adoption curve, early adopters play a crucial role in the success of a product or service. They are the adventurous risk-takers who embrace new technologies and innovations. Identifying and engaging with early adopters can lead to valuable feedback, word-of-mouth marketing, and a snowball effect that attracts the early majority and beyond.

Early adopters are crucial for several reasons:

a. Feedback and Improvements: Early adopters are more willing to provide honest feedback about a product's strengths and weaknesses. This valuable input can be used to make essential improvements and enhancements before the product reaches a wider audience.

b. Evangelists and Advocates: Satisfied early adopters often become passionate advocates for the product, spreading the word through social media, blogs, and other channels. Their enthusiasm can create a ripple effect, driving more users to try out the product.

c. Market Validation: Winning over early adopters demonstrates market validation and indicates that there is a genuine demand for the product. This validation can attract further investment and support for the startup.

Beta Launch Platforms - A Gateway to Your Audience:

Beta launch platforms offer an ideal gateway for startups to reach their target audience - the early adopters. These platforms act as intermediaries, connecting startups with users who are eager to try out and provide feedback on beta versions of products. The benefits of leveraging these platforms include:

a. Exposure to a Targeted Audience: Beta launch platforms have niche communities of tech enthusiasts and early adopters who actively seek new and innovative solutions. By featuring your product on these platforms, you gain access to a highly targeted audience interested in exploring cutting-edge technologies.

b. Access to Valuable Feedback: Early users on these platforms are often tech-savvy and passionate about new innovations. Their feedback can offer valuable insights into potential improvements, uncovering issues that may have been overlooked during development.

c. Word-of-Mouth Marketing: Positive experiences shared by early adopters can lead to organic promotion and expand your user base. These users are more likely to share their excitement with their networks, creating a snowball effect of user acquisition.

Making the Most of Beta Launch Platforms:

To maximize the impact of beta launch platforms, consider the following tips:

a. Tailor Your Messaging: Craft compelling messages that resonate with early adopters and clearly communicate the value proposition of your product. Highlight what sets your product apart and why it is relevant to the target audience.

b. Provide a Sneak Peek: Offer a glimpse into the unique features and benefits of your beta version to pique the interest of potential users. Engage their curiosity by sharing exciting aspects that encourage them to sign up for the beta.

c. Engage Actively: Participate in discussions, respond to feedback, and build relationships with users on the platform. Show that you value their input and are actively working to create a better user experience.

d. Learn from Feedback: Embrace constructive criticism and use it to refine your product before the official launch. Early adopters are often tech-savvy and can provide valuable insights that lead to significant improvements.

Leveraging the Startup Ecosystem:

Apart from beta launch platforms, explore other elements of the startup ecosystem, such as incubators, accelerators, and co-working spaces. These resources can provide invaluable support, mentorship, and networking opportunities for your startup.

a. Incubators and Accelerators: Joining an incubator or accelerator program can provide access to mentorship, funding, and a supportive community of fellow entrepreneurs.

b. Co-working Spaces: Co-working spaces offer a vibrant environment where startups can collaborate, network, and share ideas with other like-minded individuals.

c. Networking Events: Attend startup events, industry conferences, and networking meetups to connect with potential partners, investors, and customers.

Beta launch platforms act as catalysts for startups, connecting them with early adopters who are eager to explore and provide feedback on new products. Leveraging these platforms can lead to invaluable insights, word-of-mouth marketing, and a solid foundation for your go-to-market strategy. As you explore the comprehensive list of 206 beta launch sites and forums, embrace the power of the startup ecosystem and propel your startup towards success. The early adopters await, and the journey of innovation beckons!

EIGHT

SHOW UP IN PUBLIC FORUMS

While online strategies like social media, search engine optimization, and online advertising are crucial for establishing your startup's online presence, they are just the first step towards success. To truly validate your proof of concept and connect with potential customers, you need to showcase your product or service to a live audience in public forums, whether online or offline. This chapter delves into the importance of participating in public forums, identifying the right platforms, and making the most of these opportunities to propel your startup forward.

The Necessity of Live Audience Interaction:

Interacting with a live audience offers several advantages that go beyond digital interactions:

a. Real-Time Feedback: Live audiences provide immediate feedback, reactions, and questions, offering valuable insights that can guide improvements and fine-tuning.

b. Enhanced Credibility: Presenting in public forums boosts your startup's credibility and legitimacy, as you demonstrate the confidence to showcase your offering to a wider audience.

c. Networking Opportunities: Public forums enable you to connect with potential customers, partners, investors, and mentors, all under one roof.

d. Exposure and Brand Visibility: Public forums provide an opportunity to increase your brand's visibility and reach a larger audience.

Finding the Right Platforms:

Finding relevant platforms to showcase your startup is crucial for maximizing the impact of live audience interactions. Consider the following options:

a. Startup Accelerators and Incubators: Many startup accelerators and incubators host demo days where startups pitch their offerings to a live audience, including potential investors.

b. Startup Pitchfests and Hackathons: Beta launch platforms and tech forums often organize startup pitchfests and hackathons, providing opportunities to showcase your tech product or service.

c. Networking Platforms: Networking forums like BNI (Business Network International) and TiE (The Indus Entrepreneurs) offer opportunities to connect with potential customers for service-based startups.

d. Relevant Events: Identify events in your business's geographical region that align with your offering and target audience. Look for events with keynote sessions and masterclasses that can provide valuable insights.

Assessing Relevance and Value:

Before participating in any event, ask yourself the following questions:

a. Past Experience: Have you attended similar events in the past, and did they offer valuable opportunities?

b. Geographic Alignment: Is the event hosted in a region relevant to your business, or would it be beneficial for expanding your presence there?

c. Keynote and Masterclass Alignment: Are there keynote sessions or masterclasses that align with your business needs and can offer valuable insights?

d. Competitor Presence: Do you see any of your leading competitors among the list of sponsors or attendees?

e. Potential Customers: Do you expect at least 40% of the attendees to be potential customers for your product or service?

f. Future Sponsorship: Can you envision sponsoring the event in the future, indicating its value for your startup's growth?

g. Conflict with Values or Goals: Are there any terms or conditions that conflict with your business's values or goals?

h. Implementation of Insights: Do you foresee implementing insights learned from this event in your business strategy?

Preparing for Public Forums:

When registering for an event, ensure complete and professional profiling of the representatives from your organization. This includes a professional photograph and a concise description of your business offering. Prepare an elevator pitch and train every representative to synchronize their language and messaging when networking with potential customers.

Making the Most of Live Audience Interaction:

To maximize the impact of public forums, follow these strategies:

a. Practice and Rehearse: Rehearse your pitch and anticipate potential questions and feedback to respond confidently.

b. Focus on Engagement: Engage the audience actively during your presentation, encouraging questions and interaction.

c. Offer Value: Showcase the value of your product or service clearly and concisely, addressing the pain points and needs of your target audience.

d. Networking Opportunities: Network actively with other participants, investors, and mentors to build valuable connections.

e. Follow-Up: After the event, follow up with potential customers and investors, keeping the momentum alive and nurturing those relationships.

Public forums offer a unique opportunity to interact with a live audience, gather real-time feedback, and enhance your startup's credibility and visibility. By participating in relevant events, you can tap into networking opportunities, connect with potential customers, and gain valuable insights for your business. As you show up in public forums, remember to be well-prepared, engage with the audience actively, and leverage these opportunities to propel your startup towards success. Embrace the power of live audience interaction, and let your startup shine in the spotlight!

NINE

Setting Up Customer Support Processes and Managing Feature Requests

As a B2B SaaS startup, providing excellent customer support and managing feature requests is crucial for building strong relationships with your beta customers and future users. This chapter explores the importance of setting up efficient customer support processes and how to effectively manage feature requests from your customers. By addressing their queries and needs promptly, you can enhance user satisfaction and gain valuable insights to improve your product.

The Significance of Customer Support in B2B SaaS:

In the world of B2B SaaS, customer support plays a pivotal role in ensuring customer satisfaction and retention. Your beta customers and early adopters are your first brand advocates, and addressing their queries and concerns quickly is vital for building trust and loyalty. Efficient customer support processes can also lead to valuable word-of-mouth referrals and positive reviews, which can significantly impact your startup's reputation and growth.

When it comes to B2B SaaS, the relationship between your company and your customers is often long-term, extending well beyond the initial purchase. As such, maintaining excellent customer support is not just a short-term strategy for boosting sales but a long-term investment in customer success. When customers feel supported, they are more likely to become loyal customers who stick with your product, provide feedback, and even refer others to your platform.

Setting Up Customer Support Processes:

To ensure a seamless customer support experience, follow these steps:

a. Choose the Right Platform: Select a customer support platform that aligns with your startup's needs and budget. Some popular options include Freshdesk, Zendesk, Zoho Desk, and Intercom. These platforms offer ticketing systems, knowledge bases, and communication channels to manage customer inquiries effectively.

b. Train Your Support Team: Equip your support team with the necessary product knowledge and communication skills to handle customer queries professionally and efficiently. Customer support representatives should have a deep understanding of your product and be capable of troubleshooting issues effectively.

c. Create a Knowledge Base: Develop a comprehensive knowledge base with FAQs, tutorials, and guides to help customers find solutions to common issues without direct assistance. A well-maintained knowledge base can significantly reduce the number of repetitive inquiries and allow your team to focus on more complex cases.

d. Implement a Ticketing System: Use a ticketing system to categorize and prioritize customer queries, ensuring no inquiry goes unnoticed or unresolved. Assign tickets to the appropriate team members based on their expertise, ensuring timely and accurate responses.

e. Set Response Time Targets: Define response time targets for different types of queries, aiming for timely and satisfactory resolutions. Customers appreciate a prompt response, even if the issue cannot be immediately resolved.

f. Monitor and Analyze: Regularly monitor customer support metrics to identify areas for improvement and measure customer satisfaction levels. Key performance indicators (KPIs) may include average response time, ticket resolution rate, and customer feedback scores.

g. Gather Feedback: Actively seek feedback from customers about their support experience. Use surveys or follow-up emails to understand how satisfied they are with the resolution provided and if there are any areas for improvement.

Addressing Feature Requests:

Feature requests from customers can provide valuable insights into their needs and preferences. Here's how to effectively manage and address feature requests:

a. Create a Dedicated Feature Request Page: Set up a dedicated page on your website where customers can submit feature requests. Consider using a WordPress feature request plugin to streamline the process. This page should be easily accessible and user-friendly to encourage customers to share their ideas.

b. Categorize and Prioritize: Categorize feature requests based on their relevance and potential impact on your product. Prioritize requests that align with your product roadmap and overall strategy. Some feature requests may be more complex or require significant development effort, so it's essential to assess the feasibility and impact of each request.

c. Gather Feedback from Your Team: Collaborate with your development and product teams to assess the feasibility and implications of implementing each feature request. Input from different departments can help evaluate the technical feasibility, potential impact on existing features, and alignment with your product vision.

d. Communicate with Customers: Keep customers informed about the status of their feature requests. Transparency and open communication can foster a positive relationship with your users. Let them know whether a feature request is under consideration, planned for development, or not feasible at the moment. Providing regular updates can demonstrate that you value their input and are actively working to improve your product.

e. Consider Beta Testing: For major feature requests, consider inviting customers to participate in a beta testing phase to gather real-world feedback before a full-scale release. Beta testing can help you fine-tune the feature based on user feedback and identify any potential issues or bugs before the official launch.

Automating Customer Support and CRM Integration:
As your B2B SaaS startup grows, manual customer support processes may become overwhelming. To maintain efficiency, consider automating customer support tasks through chatbots, automated responses, and ticket assignment workflows. Additionally, integrate your customer support system with your CRM to ensure seamless communication and data sharing between teams.

a. Implementing Chatbots: Chatbots can handle routine queries, such as password resets or account information updates, 24/7, reducing the burden on your support team and providing quick responses to customers.

b. Automated Responses: Set up automated responses for common inquiries, acknowledging the receipt of the customer's query and informing them about the expected response time. This automated acknowledgment reassures customers that their request is being attended to.

c. Ticket Assignment Workflows: Design ticket assignment workflows to ensure that customer queries are routed to the most appropriate team member based on their expertise. This avoids unnecessary delays and ensures that queries are handled by the best-suited support representative.

d. CRM Integration: Integrate your customer support system with your CRM to maintain a centralized customer database. This integration allows your support team to access relevant customer information and interactions, enabling them to provide personalized assistance.

e. Leveraging AI and Machine Learning: Implement AI-powered solutions to analyze support interactions, identify patterns, and recommend potential solutions to support representatives. AI-driven insights can help improve response times and overall support quality.

Managing B2C Offering at Scale:

For large-scale B2C offerings with up to 1000 beta users, manual support becomes impractical. Implement marketing automation systems and a robust CRM before opening up the beta. Utilize segmentation and personalized communication to manage the customer journey effectively and provide relevant support.

a. Segmentation: Segment your beta users based on their behavior, preferences, and engagement levels. This segmentation enables targeted communication and personalized support for different groups of users.

b. Automated Onboarding: Implement automated onboarding processes for new beta users, providing them with a guided experience to explore your product's features and functionalities.

c. Personalized Communication: Use personalized email marketing and in-app messaging to communicate with your beta users. Address them by their names and tailor messages to their specific needs and interests.

d. Support Knowledge Base: Create an extensive support knowledge base that covers frequently asked questions and common troubleshooting steps. Beta users can access this self-help resource, reducing the need for direct support interactions.

e. Social Media and Community Management: Engage with your beta users on social media platforms and create a community where users can connect, share feedback, and support one another.

Leveraging Feedback for Product Improvement:

Customer support interactions and feature requests provide a wealth of feedback that can be invaluable for product improvement and iteration. Here's how to effectively leverage customer feedback:

a. Regular Feedback Reviews: Conduct regular reviews of customer feedback with your product and development teams. Analyze recurring issues, pain points, and popular feature requests to inform product development priorities.

b. Feature Prioritization: Use customer feedback to prioritize feature development. Understanding which features are in high demand or have the potential to drive user satisfaction can guide your product roadmap.

c. User Testing: Involve beta users in user testing sessions for new features or significant product updates. Gather real-world insights and observe how users interact with your product to identify areas for improvement.

d. Customer Feedback Surveys: Send out customer feedback surveys to gauge overall satisfaction and identify areas where your product and support can be enhanced.

e. Customer Success Stories: Celebrate customer success stories and use them as testimonials to demonstrate the value of your product to potential users.

Setting up robust customer support processes and effectively managing feature requests is vital for the success of your B2B SaaS startup. By promptly addressing customer queries, providing top-notch support, and valuing their feature requests, you can strengthen customer relationships, build brand loyalty, and foster positive word-of-mouth. Additionally, integrating automation and CRM systems streamlines support operations and enhances overall efficiency. Embrace customer-centricity and make support and feature request management cornerstones of your startup's growth strategy, propelling your B2B SaaS offering to new heights of success. In the ever-evolving world of technology, a company's customer support processes are more critical than ever. The level of support you offer can significantly impact your company's reputation, customer satisfaction, and ultimately, your bottom line.

By following the guidelines and best practices outlined in this chapter, you can create a customer support system that meets and exceeds the expectations of your users. The key is to remain proactive, responsive, and attentive to customer needs. Take customer feedback seriously and use it to continuously improve your product and service offerings. In doing so, you'll not only retain existing customers but also attract new ones through positive word-of-mouth and referrals. Customer support is an ongoing process that requires continuous monitoring and improvement. By investing in your customer support team and processes, you're investing in the long-term success of your B2B SaaS startup.

TEN

PREPARING TECHNICAL DOCUMENTATION

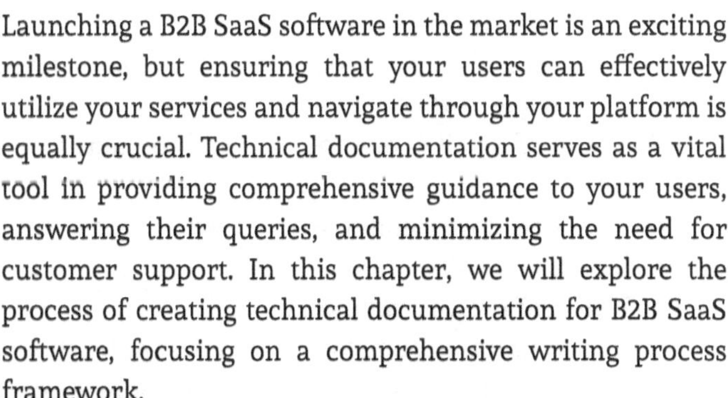

Launching a B2B SaaS software in the market is an exciting milestone, but ensuring that your users can effectively utilize your services and navigate through your platform is equally crucial. Technical documentation serves as a vital tool in providing comprehensive guidance to your users, answering their queries, and minimizing the need for customer support. In this chapter, we will explore the process of creating technical documentation for B2B SaaS software, focusing on a comprehensive writing process framework.

The Importance of Technical Documentation:

Technical documentation plays a pivotal role in enabling users to understand and leverage your B2B SaaS software effectively. A well-crafted documentation acts as a knowledge transfer mechanism within teams and provides end-to-end explanations of how to use your business offering. Clear and accessible documentation enhances the user experience, reduces support tickets, and fosters customer satisfaction.

Understanding Your Users and Their Needs:

Before diving into the writing process, it is essential to understand your target audience and their specific needs. Your users come from various backgrounds, expertise levels, and industries.

Identifying their pain points and requirements will help you tailor the technical documentation to their specific use cases, ensuring maximum value from your platform.

Defining the Objectives of Your Technical Documentation:

Before you start writing, set clear objectives for your technical documentation. Ask yourself the following questions:

What are the key features and functionalities of your B2B SaaS software that users need to know about?

How can your documentation address common user challenges and queries?

What level of detail should be provided to guide users effectively?

How will the documentation align with your overall brand identity and voice?

The Writing Process Framework:

Creating technical documentation requires a structured approach to ensure that your content is comprehensive, accurate, and user-friendly.

The following framework outlines the essential steps in the writing process:

Step 1: Plan the Document's Content:

Begin by outlining what should be covered in the documentation. The table of contents (ToC) serves as a roadmap for the document and helps you maintain a logical sequence of topics. Consider what tasks users will perform on your platform and how they should navigate through it. Ensure that your team is well-informed about the typical customer journey on your platform before starting the documentation process.

Step 2: Define a Schema for Topics:

The schema acts as a template for each topic listed in the table of contents. This standardized format ensures that all relevant aspects are covered consistently throughout the documentation. Each topic should include the following sections:

Title: Clearly indicate the topic, feature, or screen you are covering.

Subtitle: Provide additional insights and the goal of the topic.

Overview: Explain what users will learn from the topic and the level of proficiency they will gain.

Walkthrough: Break down each section, feature, or page and explain how users can work with it step-by-step.

Read Next: Provide a link to the next topic in the logical sequence.

By following this schema, you can ensure that your documentation is user-friendly and easy to navigate, promoting cognitive fluency and making it easier for users to utilize your platform effectively.

Step 3: Create Content:

With the schema in place, creating content becomes more manageable. Focus on filling in the subtitle, overview, and walkthrough for each topic.

Utilize screenshots to visually guide users through the process, ensuring clarity and ease of understanding. Consider embedding related help videos on the same page to provide additional visual support.

Step 4: Review and Revise:

Once the content is drafted, conduct thorough reviews to ensure accuracy, clarity, and completeness. Involve multiple stakeholders, including team members and beta users, to gather feedback and make necessary revisions. Iterative reviews will help refine the documentation and address potential gaps.

Step 5: Incorporate User Feedback:

Technical documentation should be a living document that evolves with user feedback and platform updates. Encourage users to provide feedback on the documentation and their experience with your platform. Use this input to identify areas for improvement and incorporate user-generated content such as FAQs, tips, and best practices.

Step 6: Organize and Format:

Present the information in a visually appealing and structured manner. Use headings, bullet points, and lists to break down complex information into digestible chunks. Ensure consistency in language and tone to maintain a seamless user experience.

Step 7: Accessible and Searchable:

Make your technical documentation easily accessible to users by integrating it into your website or platform's help center. Implement a search functionality to allow users to quickly find the specific information they need.

Engaging and Supporting Your Users:

Creating technical documentation is just the beginning. To engage and support your users effectively, consider the following strategies:

a. User Onboarding: Implement a user onboarding process that guides new users through your platform's features and functionalities. Offer guided tours and tutorials to help users get started and become proficient with your software.

b. Regular Updates: Keep your documentation up to date with the latest features and improvements to your platform. Regularly review and update the content to ensure accuracy and relevance.

c. Support Community: Establish a support community where users can interact, share experiences, and help one another. Active community engagement can foster a sense of belonging and provide valuable insights for product improvements.

d. Feedback Mechanism: Encourage users to provide feedback on the documentation and platform usability. Use their input to identify pain points, address gaps in the documentation, and enhance the overall user experience.

e. Multichannel Support: Offer multichannel support options, such as chat, email, and phone, to accommodate various user preferences and ensure prompt responses to queries.

User-Centric Approach:

Keep in mind that technical documentation is a means to empower your users. Adopt a user-centric approach by considering their needs, preferences, and pain points. Use customer feedback and support interactions to identify areas for improvement and refine your documentation accordingly.

Leveraging Documentation for Marketing:

Technical documentation can serve as a marketing asset, showcasing the features and capabilities of your B2B SaaS software. Use snippets of documentation in your marketing materials, website, and social media to demonstrate the value and usability of your platform.

Creating technical documentation for your B2B SaaS software is a crucial step in enabling users to make the most of your platform. By planning the content, defining a schema, and creating user-friendly material, you can empower users to navigate your platform confidently. Comprehensive documentation reduces the need for customer support and fosters positive user experiences. Engage and support your users through onboarding, a support community, and a feedback mechanism. Adopt a user-centric approach, and leverage documentation as a marketing asset to showcase your platform's features and capabilities. By prioritizing technical documentation, you can enhance customer satisfaction, build long-lasting relationships, and drive the success of your B2B SaaS startup.

ELEVEN

CREATING EFFECTIVE VIDEOS

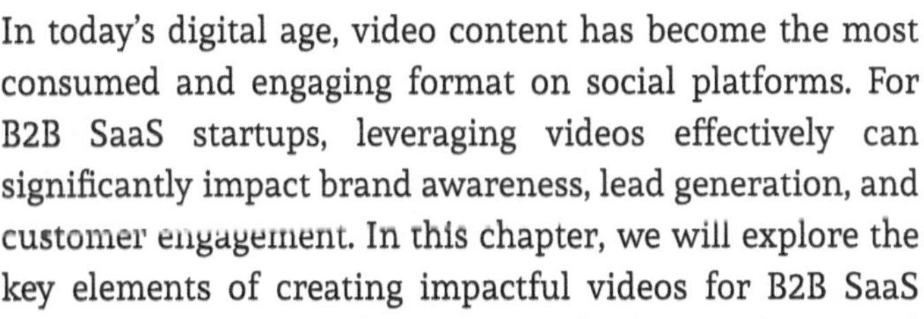

In today's digital age, video content has become the most consumed and engaging format on social platforms. For B2B SaaS startups, leveraging videos effectively can significantly impact brand awareness, lead generation, and customer engagement. In this chapter, we will explore the key elements of creating impactful videos for B2B SaaS startups, including different types of videos and essential production checklist.

The Science of Videos:

Videos have the unique ability to convey complex information in a visually compelling and easily digestible format. They evoke emotions, tell stories, and establish a genuine connection with the audience. For B2B SaaS startups, videos can play a crucial role in building brand credibility, demonstrating product features, providing tutorials, and showcasing success stories.

Different Types of Videos for B2B SaaS Startups:

When creating videos for your B2B SaaS startup, it is essential to diversify your content strategy to cater to different stages of the buyer's journey.

Here are the three key types of videos to consider:

a. Hub Content:

Hub content focuses on your brand and its core aspects. These videos have the primary goal of promoting brand authenticity and showcasing your company's values, vision, and achievements. Hub content can include the following:

Brand Story: Tell the story of how your B2B SaaS startup came into existence, the challenges you faced, and the solutions you offer. This helps establish an emotional connection with your audience and builds trust.

Event Recordings: Capture the highlights of important events, conferences, webinars, or product launches your company hosts or participates in. Share these recordings to demonstrate thought leadership and industry expertise.

Product Catalogs: Showcase your range of products and services in a visually appealing manner. Highlight key features and use cases to attract potential customers and encourage them to explore further.

Feature Demonstrations: Provide detailed demonstrations of specific features or functionalities of your SaaS platform. This helps users understand how your product can address their pain points and streamline their workflow.

b. Help Content:

Help content involves creating a series of videos grouped into playlists, addressing specific topics or providing how-to guides related to your area of expertise.

This type of content is focused on educating your audience, offering solutions to their challenges, and positioning your B2B SaaS startup as an industry expert. Help content can include the following:

Tutorials: Create step-by-step tutorials that guide users on how to use your SaaS platform effectively. These tutorials can cover onboarding processes, account setup, and various tasks that users might encounter.

Tips and Tricks: Share valuable tips, shortcuts, and best practices that can enhance the user experience and productivity of your platform. These videos demonstrate your commitment to customer success.

Use Cases: Highlight real-world use cases and success stories of existing customers who have benefited from using your SaaS solution. This helps build social proof and credibility among potential customers.

c. Hero Content:

Hero content aims to create potential viral material that captures the attention of a broader audience and drives brand recognition. This type of video content often involves a compelling story, creative storytelling, and high production value. Hero content can include the following:

Brand Commercials: Develop short, attention-grabbing commercials that showcase the unique selling points of your B2B SaaS startup. These commercials should be emotionally resonant and memorable.

Thought Leadership: Create thought-provoking videos that address industry challenges, trends, and innovations. Position your company's executives or subject matter experts as thought leaders in the industry.

Trending Topics: Capitalize on trending topics or current events that align with your brand's values and offerings. Engage with your audience by providing relevant insights and perspectives on these topics.

Key Elements of Video Production:

While creating videos, it is crucial to pay attention to various elements to ensure high-quality and engaging content. Here is a checklist for video production:

a. Location and Setting:

Select appropriate locations for the shoot that align with your video's theme and message. Ensure the setting complements your brand's identity and conveys the desired atmosphere.

b. Lighting:

Proper lighting is essential for video production. Choose lighting setups that enhance visibility and clarity, avoiding harsh shadows or overexposure.

c. Dress Code:

Ensure that the people featured in the video follow a suitable dress code that reflects your brand's image and professionalism.

d. Equipment:

Determine the number of cameras, drones, and gimbals required for capturing different angles and perspectives. Investing in quality equipment can significantly improve the overall video quality.

e. Post-Production Setup:

During post-production, add animated graphics at the beginning and end of the video. This helps reinforce your brand's visual identity and provides a professional touch.

f. Green Background:

Consider using a green background for composite layering during post-production, allowing you to add graphics or change backgrounds seamlessly. While optional, this technique can enhance the visual appeal of your videos.

Video Production Process:

To ensure a smooth and effective video production process, follow these steps:

a. Pre-Production Planning:

Plan your video content, script, locations, equipment, and talent well in advance. A detailed pre-production plan saves time, minimizes errors, and enhances overall efficiency.

b. Script Development:

Write a compelling script that aligns with your video's objective and resonates with your target audience. Keep the script concise, engaging, and action-oriented.

c. Production:

Execute the video shoot according to the pre-defined plan. Pay attention to camera angles, lighting, and audio quality during the shoot.

d. Post-Production Editing:

Edit the footage, add animations, and enhance the overall visual appeal during post-production. Use editing software to refine the video and ensure a polished final product.

Leveraging Videos for Marketing:

After creating impactful videos, leverage them strategically for marketing purposes. While the How-Tos are explorable, consider the below elements as a checklist for you to kickstart your efforts:

a. YouTube Channel:

Create a dedicated YouTube channel for your B2B SaaS startup and organize videos into relevant playlists. Optimize video titles, descriptions, and tags for better visibility.

b. Website Integration:

Embed videos on your website's landing pages, blog posts, and product pages. Videos can enhance user engagement and increase time spent on your site.

c. Social Media Promotion:

Share videos on social media platforms, such as LinkedIn, Twitter, and Facebook, to reach a wider audience and generate brand awareness.

d. Email Marketing:

Include video content in your email marketing campaigns to increase click-through rates and engagement.

e. Webinars and Events:

Use videos as part of webinars and events to enhance presentations, educate participants, and engage with your audience.

Videos are a powerful tool for B2B SaaS startups to engage with their audience, showcase product features, and build brand credibility. Understanding the different types of videos and following a comprehensive production checklist can result in high-quality and impactful content. By strategically leveraging videos across various marketing channels, B2B SaaS startups can amplify their reach, drive user engagement, and achieve long-term success in the competitive digital landscape. Invest in video production, tell your brand story, educate your audience, and leave a lasting impression on potential customers through the power of compelling visual content.

TWELVE

FIXING YOUR P R STRATEGY

In the fast-paced and highly competitive world of B2B SaaS startups, having a well-crafted PR strategy is critical to gaining visibility, credibility, and market traction. Public relations play a pivotal role in building brand recognition, establishing thought leadership, and fostering trust among potential customers and industry experts. In this chapter, we will delve deeper into the nuances of crafting an effective PR strategy specifically tailored for B2B SaaS startups.

Understanding the Distinct Differences: B2C vs. B2B PR Strategy

While both B2C and B2B PR strategies aim to connect with target audiences and enhance brand perception, the approaches are markedly different. B2B SaaS startups cater to businesses and professionals, and their PR efforts revolve around building industry authority, showcasing expertise, and fostering long-term relationships.

Unlike B2C, where mass appeal and emotional resonance are often paramount, B2B PR focuses on providing valuable insights, thought leadership, and solutions to address specific business challenges.

Key Questions to Craft a Successful PR Strategy:

Which Region Are You Targeting?

Identifying the specific regions where your B2B SaaS startup aims to establish a strong presence is crucial. Consider the geographical scope of your target market and tailor your PR efforts accordingly.

Localizing your messaging and engaging with regional media outlets can amplify your brand's visibility within your target audience.

Who are the Key Beneficiaries of Your B2B Offering?

Defining your ideal customer profile is fundamental to crafting an effective PR strategy. Understand the pain points, needs, and aspirations of your target customers to tailor your messages and content to resonate with their interests.

What Media Outlets do Your Beneficiaries Engage with?

Thoroughly research the media outlets, publications, and online platforms that your target customers regularly engage with. B2B SaaS startups should focus on industry-specific publications, trade journals, and online forums where decision-makers seek industry insights and solutions.

Network with Reporters and Journalists:

Building strong relationships with reporters, journalists, and industry influencers is instrumental in securing media coverage and thought leadership opportunities. Attend industry events, conferences, and networking forums to engage with relevant media professionals.

How do You Want to Deliver Your Message?

Determine the most effective channels to deliver your PR messages and thought leadership content. B2B SaaS startups can leverage a mix of traditional PR (press releases, media interviews) and digital platforms (social media, content marketing, webinars) to reach their target audience.

Crafting a Compelling Press Release:

A press release is a key element of any PR strategy, serving as a formal announcement of company news, product launches, or business milestones. To make your press releases compelling and effective:

Keep it concise and focused: Stick to the word limit, typically around 400 words, and focus on the key message you want to convey.

Use the Three-Paragraph Format: Follow the standard press release structure, including the release time and date, the main message in the first paragraph, relevant details in the second paragraph, and a brief conclusion in the third paragraph.

Timeliness is Crucial: Most press releases are intended for immediate release, so ensure your content is timely and relevant to the current market trends.

Orchestrating a Targeted PR Outreach:

For B2B SaaS startups, a targeted PR outreach is essential to create a lasting impact and generate valuable leads. Consider the following activities as part of your PR strategy:

Thought Leadership Content:

Establish your expertise and prowess in the industry by developing high-quality thought leadership content that addresses key industry challenges and offers valuable insights.

Publish articles, whitepapers, research reports, and videos & podcasts on reputable industry platforms to establish your startup as a trusted authority.

Industry Webinars and Podcasts:

Host webinars and participate in podcasts to share expertise, showcase your product's capabilities, and engage with industry leaders. These interactive platforms offer a unique opportunity to connect with potential customers and build industry relationships.

Customer Case Studies:

Highlight success stories and customer testimonials through case studies that demonstrate the effectiveness of your B2B SaaS solution. Publish these case studies on your website and share them with relevant media outlets for additional exposure.

Speaking Engagements at Industry Events:

Secure speaking engagements at industry conferences, seminars, and virtual events to showcase your startup's expertise and share valuable insights with a captive audience.

Crafting a successful PR strategy is essential for B2B SaaS startups to navigate the competitive landscape, build brand reputation, and attract potential customers. By understanding the nuances of B2B PR, answering critical questions, and developing compelling press releases, startups can effectively engage with their target audience and position themselves as industry leaders. Embrace a well-orchestrated and targeted PR outreach, leverage digital platforms, and foster strong relationships with industry influencers to drive sustained growth and success for your B2B SaaS startup. Remember, effective PR is about building credibility, trust, and meaningful connections within your target market, and that requires a strategic and thoughtful approach to your PR efforts.

THIRTEEN

GETTING BETA USERS' FEEDBACK

Further to opening up private beta as discussed in the fifth chapter, this chapter details on how to make effective use of the feedback from your private beta and further leveraging beta launch platforms to attract early users for your B2B SaaS startup.

Now, it's time to harness the valuable feedback from these beta users to fine-tune your business offering and cater to their specific needs effectively. In this chapter, we will explore the essential steps to collect and analyze feedback from your beta users, understand their requirements, and make data-driven decisions to enhance your product or service.

Building Strong Communication Channels:

To effectively gather feedback from beta users, establish clear and accessible communication channels. Offer multiple touchpoints such as email, chat support, dedicated forums, and feature request pages. Encourage users to provide candid feedback and make them feel valued by responding promptly to their queries and suggestions.

Feedback vs. Testimonials:

While testimonials can be valuable for marketing purposes, the focus of beta user feedback should be on understanding their needs, pain points, and expectations from your business offering. Instead of asking for testimonials, seek feedback on specific aspects such as feature requests, user experience, and potential improvements.

Identifying Common Themes:

As feedback starts pouring in, carefully analyze and categorize the responses to identify common themes. Look for recurring feature requests, pain points, and suggestions for improvement. These common themes will provide insights into the most pressing needs of your target audience.

Integrating with Third-Party Systems:

Pay close attention to beta users' mentions of using other systems or tools that can be integrated with your SaaS platform. Identifying integration opportunities can open up possibilities for partnerships and value-added services, enhancing the overall user experience.

Aligning with Roadmap:

Compare the feedback received with your existing product roadmap. Determine if the requests align with your long-term vision for the product. Prioritize features and enhancements based on their potential impact on user satisfaction and the scalability of your business offering.

Distinguishing Support Issues from Feature Requests:

Some beta users may report technical issues or challenges they are facing while using your platform. Separate these support issues from feature requests to ensure timely resolution of critical problems while also addressing new feature demands.

Leveraging Customer Support and Feature Request Pages:

Encourage beta users to utilize your customer support system for issue resolution. This will not only address their concerns promptly but also provide you with valuable insights into common pain points. Create a dedicated feature request page where beta users can submit their suggestions and ideas for new features or enhancements. This crowdsourcing approach empowers users to actively participate in shaping the future of your product while providing you with a wealth of creative input.

The Power of Data-Driven Decisions:

Collecting feedback from beta users and analyzing it in a structured manner empowers your B2B SaaS startup to make data-driven decisions. Use the insights gained to prioritize development efforts, allocate resources efficiently, and align your product roadmap with market demand.

Iterative Feedback Loop:

Feedback collection should not be a one-time event but an ongoing process. Continuously engage with beta users, monitor their experiences, and seek feedback on new iterations of your product. Implementing an iterative feedback loop ensures your business offering remains relevant and responsive to evolving customer needs.

Importance of Engaging with Beta Users:

The beta testing phase is a crucial opportunity to build strong relationships with your early adopters. Engaging with beta users not only enables you to identify product improvements but also fosters a sense of ownership and loyalty among users. Acknowledge their contributions, express gratitude, and make them feel part of the product development journey.

Feedback Analytics and Sentiment Analysis:

Leverage data analytics tools to analyze the feedback collected from beta users. Sentiment analysis can help you gauge user satisfaction levels and identify areas that require immediate attention. Utilize qualitative and quantitative data to draw actionable insights for product enhancement and marketing strategies.

Implementing User Feedback:

As you receive valuable feedback, prioritize the most requested features and improvements. Implementing user feedback and showcasing how their input has influenced product development reinforces the trust and credibility of your business offering. Keep your beta users informed about the progress and updates they can expect.

Building a Community:

Create a community for your beta users to interact with each other, share experiences, and provide peer support. A vibrant community fosters user engagement and loyalty, encouraging beta users to become brand advocates.

Continuous Improvement through Beta Phases:

Consider running multiple beta phases to refine your product based on iterative feedback. Each beta phase allows you to gather more data, identify new use cases, and address additional pain points.

This cyclical approach to beta testing ensures continuous improvement and positions your B2B SaaS startup for long-term success.

Collaboration with Early Adopters:

Engage your early adopters in collaborative discussions and seek their insights on potential roadblocks and improvements.

Co-create solutions with them, aligning your business offering with their needs and expectations.

Monitoring Competitor Feedback:
Keep a close eye on feedback and reviews of your competitors' products in the market. Understanding what customers appreciate and dislike about competing offerings can provide valuable pointers for your product's positioning and differentiation.

Effective beta user feedback is a powerful tool for fine-tuning your B2B SaaS startup's product or service. Building strong communication channels, identifying common themes, leveraging customer support and feature request pages, and implementing a data-driven approach will help you harness valuable insights from your beta users. Engaging with beta users, building a community, and collaboratively addressing pain points position your startup for success in a competitive market. Remember, the journey of improvement and innovation is ongoing, and your beta users will be your valuable partners in this exciting venture.

FOURTEEN

IDENTIFYING MARKETING CHANNELS

As a B2B SaaS startup, your success depends on reaching the right audience through the most effective marketing channels. The process of identifying these channels requires a deep understanding of your target customers, their behavior, and the competitive landscape. In this comprehensive guide, we will explore advanced strategies to help you choose the most suitable marketing channels to drive growth and maximize your return on investment (ROI).

Conduct In-Depth Market Research:

Before diving into marketing channels, conduct thorough market research to gain insights into your target audience and industry. Use both primary and secondary research methods to gather data, including surveys, interviews, competitor analysis, and market reports. Understanding your customers' pain points, preferences, and buying behavior will be instrumental in determining the most effective marketing channels.

Start by defining your target market segments and understanding their specific needs and challenges. This will help you tailor your marketing messages and strategies to resonate with each segment. Additionally, research your competitors to identify their marketing tactics and understand the gaps in the market that you can capitalize on.

Define Clear Marketing Objectives:

Establish specific, measurable, achievable, relevant, and time-bound (SMART) marketing objectives. Your objectives should align with your overall business goals and provide a clear direction for your marketing efforts.

Examples of marketing objectives for B2B SaaS startups include lead generation, customer acquisition, brand awareness, and customer retention.

Once you have defined your objectives, prioritize them based on their importance and impact on your business.

This will help you allocate resources effectively and focus on the channels that will drive the most significant results.

Develop a Comprehensive Buyer Persona:

Creating detailed buyer personas is essential for effective marketing channel selection. Define the characteristics, preferences, challenges, and goals of your ideal customers. Use these personas to guide your marketing strategies and tailor your messaging to resonate with your target audience.

To create accurate buyer personas, conduct interviews and surveys with your existing customers to gather valuable insights into their motivations and pain points. Additionally, leverage data analytics to analyze customer behavior and identify patterns and trends that can inform your persona development.

Analyze Customer Journey:

Map out the customer journey to understand the touchpoints where potential customers interact with your brand. Identify the key stages, pain points, and decision-making criteria during their journey. This analysis will help you identify the most relevant marketing channels for each stage of the buyer's journey.

At each stage of the customer journey, consider the different marketing channels that can effectively engage and influence your target audience.

For example, content marketing and thought leadership can be powerful channels for attracting prospects during the awareness stage, while email marketing and webinars can nurture leads during the consideration stage.

Leverage Data Analytics:

Data analytics is critical in assessing the performance of different marketing channels. Utilize web analytics tools, such as Google Analytics, to track user behavior, traffic sources, conversion rates, and other key metrics. Use this data to optimize your marketing efforts and allocate resources to high-performing channels.

In addition to web analytics, leverage marketing automation platforms to track the performance of your email campaigns, social media efforts, and other marketing initiatives. Use A/B testing to experiment with different strategies and identify the most effective approaches for achieving your marketing objectives.

Content Marketing:

Content marketing is a cornerstone of B2B SaaS marketing. Create high-quality, informative content that addresses your audience's pain points, educates them about your product, and showcases your expertise.

Consider various content formats, including blog posts, e-books, infographics, videos, and webinars, to engage your audience.

Develop a content calendar that aligns with your marketing objectives and buyer personas. Create content that is relevant to each stage of the buyer's journey, from educational content for the awareness stage to product-focused content for the decision stage.

Thought Leadership and Industry Networking:

Quite iterative as it gets. I may be repeating this in the upcoming chapters too. Position your brand as a thought leader in the industry by contributing to industry publications, participating in webinars, and speaking at conferences.

Build relationships with industry influencers and peers to expand your reach and gain credibility.

Thought leadership can be a powerful marketing channel for B2B SaaS startups to establish authority and trust in their target market.

Consider hosting webinars and virtual events to share your expertise and engage with potential customers in real-time.

Account-Based Marketing (ABM):

ABM is a highly targeted approach that focuses on personalized marketing to individual accounts. Tailor your content and messaging to address the specific needs and pain points of target accounts. Use account-based advertising and direct outreach to engage key decision-makers.

ABM is particularly effective for B2B SaaS startups that target enterprise-level clients. By focusing on individual accounts, you can deliver highly personalized marketing messages that resonate with decision-makers and influencers within the organization.

Social Media Marketing:

Leverage social media platforms, such as LinkedIn, Twitter, and Facebook, to connect with your target audience and build brand awareness. Engage in industry-specific groups and discussions to showcase your expertise and connect with potential customers.

Choose social media platforms that align with your target audience's preferences and behavior. For example, LinkedIn is a valuable platform for B2B SaaS startups to connect with professionals and decision-makers in their industry.

Search Engine Optimization (SEO):

Optimize your website and content to improve organic search rankings and visibility. Conduct keyword research to identify relevant search terms used by your target audience.

Create valuable content that aligns with search intent and build high-quality backlinks to improve domain authority.

SEO is a long-term strategy that requires continuous monitoring and optimization. Regularly analyze your website's performance in search results and make adjustments to improve your rankings and visibility.

Pay-Per-Click (PPC) Advertising:

PPC advertising allows you to target specific keywords and demographics to reach your ideal customers. Use platforms like Google Ads and LinkedIn Ads to run targeted PPC campaigns and drive qualified traffic to your website.

Set clear objectives for your PPC campaigns, such as lead generation or customer acquisition, and monitor their performance closely.

Optimize your ad copy, landing pages, and targeting parameters to maximize the ROI of your PPC campaigns.

Email Marketing:

Segment your email lists based on customer behavior and preferences. Implement personalized email campaigns to nurture leads, engage with potential customers, and drive conversions.

Email marketing is an effective channel for building relationships with your audience and staying top-of-mind with potential customers. Use automation to send personalized emails based on user behavior, such as abandoned cart emails or re-engagement campaigns.

Webinars and Virtual Events:

Organize webinars and virtual events to showcase your product's capabilities, present thought leadership content, and engage with potential customers in real-time.

Webinars are a valuable channel for educating your audience about your product and industry trends. Consider partnering with industry influencers or complementary businesses to co-host webinars and expand your reach.

Partner Marketing and Influencer Collaborations:

Collaborate with industry influencers and complementary businesses to extend your reach and tap into their existing customer base. Consider creating co-branded content and joint marketing initiatives.

Partner marketing and influencer collaborations can help your B2B SaaS startup reach new audiences and gain credibility in the market.

Identify influencers and partners with a strong presence in your industry and align with your brand values.

Referral Programs:

Implement a customer referral program to incentivize satisfied customers to refer your product to their networks.

Offer rewards for successful referrals to boost customer acquisition.

Referral programs are a cost-effective way to leverage your existing customer base to generate new leads. Create clear guidelines and incentives for referrals and track the performance of your referral program to measure its impact on your customer acquisition efforts.

Identifying the most effective marketing channels for your B2B SaaS startup requires a data-driven, customer-centric approach. By conducting in-depth market research, defining clear marketing objectives, and understanding your target audience's behavior, you can develop a comprehensive marketing strategy that aligns with your business goals. Leverage content marketing, thought leadership, social media, SEO, PPC advertising, email marketing, webinars, and other channels to reach your target customers at different stages of the buyer's journey. Continuously analyze and optimize your marketing efforts based on data insights to drive sustainable growth and success in the competitive B2B SaaS market. Remember, choosing the right marketing channels is not a one-time decision; it requires ongoing evaluation and adaptation to stay ahead of the competition and achieve long-term success.

FIFTEEN

STRATEGIC APPROACH TO SET THE PERFECT LAUNCH DATE

In the fast-paced world of B2B SaaS startups, the timing of your product launch can significantly impact its success. A well-planned and strategically executed launch can create a buzz in the market, attract early adopters, and establish your brand's presence. On the other hand, a rushed or poorly timed launch can lead to missed opportunities and potential setbacks.

The Three Week Theory, a concept designed to plan and execute activities over a three-week period, provides a framework to prepare for your product launch effectively. As you approach this critical phase of your startup journey, it becomes crucial to consider various parameters and make informed decisions that align with your business goals.

This chapter delves deep into the process of setting the perfect launch date for your B2B SaaS startup. It explores advanced strategies and insights, taking into account the nuances specific to the B2B SaaS industry. From technical preparations and customer feedback to crafting a comprehensive go-to-market strategy and ensuring scalability, each step plays a pivotal role in orchestrating a successful launch.

1. Preparation of Help Contents and Assets

Beyond the brilliance of your software, a smooth and successful product launch requires thorough preparation of help contents and assets. Help content, including technical documentation, tutorial videos, and pitch decks, is essential for guiding users in effectively using your platform. While creating awareness is vital, offering comprehensive support and guidance can boost user adoption and minimize the burden on customer support.

Advanced Tip: Implement intelligent help features, such as in-app contextual guidance and interactive tutorials, to enhance the user onboarding experience.

2. Leveraging Feedback from Beta Users

Beta users are invaluable assets during the private beta phase. Their feedback and insights offer critical guidance for refining your product before the public launch. It is essential to carefully analyze and evaluate the feedback received, identifying common pain points and valuable feature requests.

Advanced Tip: Engage with beta users in interactive feedback sessions or virtual focus groups to gain deeper insights into their needs and expectations.

3. Formulating a Comprehensive Go-To-Market Strategy

A well-crafted go-to-market (GTM) strategy is key to reaching and engaging your target audience effectively. Advanced B2B SaaS startups recognize the importance of integrated marketing efforts, encompassing social media campaigns, email marketing, content marketing, and account-based marketing (ABM) strategies.

Advanced Tip: Leverage data-driven insights to tailor personalized messaging and target decision-makers within your potential customer organizations.

4. Rigorous Testing and Quality Assurance

Thorough testing and quality assurance are essential before the product launch to ensure a seamless user experience. Advanced B2B SaaS startups conduct extensive testing across different platforms, devices, and user scenarios.

Advanced Tip: Implement continuous testing and deployment practices, such as DevOps and automated testing, to maintain agility and deliver frequent updates.

5. Ensuring Scalability and Infrastructure Readiness

A successful product launch can lead to a surge in user traffic. Ensuring that your infrastructure is scalable and prepared to handle increased demand is crucial to prevent performance issues and maintain user satisfaction.

Advanced Tip: Explore cloud-based solutions and containerization to achieve flexible and scalable infrastructure, adapting to fluctuating user demands.

6. Compliance and Legal Considerations

Compliance with legal and regulatory requirements is critical in the B2B SaaS industry. Advanced startups thoroughly identify and adhere to relevant laws, licenses, and agreements to avoid potential legal complications.

Advanced Tip: Collaborate with legal experts and consultants to ensure comprehensive compliance with data privacy and industry-specific regulations.

7. Setting Realistic Goals and Milestones

Strategic B2B SaaS startups set measurable and achievable goals for their product launch. These goals are aligned with the target market, competition, and industry trends, providing a basis for measuring success and making data-driven decisions.

Advanced Tip: Implement data analytics and performance tracking tools to monitor KPIs and gain real-time insights into launch progress.

8. Coordinating with Stakeholders

If your launch involves collaboration with partners or external stakeholders, streamlined communication and coordination are critical. Advanced startups build strong partnerships and establish clear roles and responsibilities to ensure a seamless and synchronized launch.

Advanced Tip: Implement partner relationship management (PRM) solutions to streamline collaboration and drive partner success.

As you navigate the complex world of B2B SaaS startups, setting the perfect launch date requires strategic planning and meticulous execution. Advanced B2B SaaS startups go beyond basic preparations and embrace data-driven insights, intelligent help features, and agile development practices to ensure a seamless and successful product launch. By leveraging feedback from beta users, formulating comprehensive go-to-market strategies, and prioritizing scalability and compliance, you can position your startup for a remarkable launch that lays the foundation for long-term success in the competitive SaaS landscape.

SIXTEEN

FOCUS ON BRANDING - BUILDING A STRONG IDENTITY

In the ever-evolving landscape of B2B SaaS startups, standing out from the crowd is more critical than ever. Amidst fierce competition, creating a strong and memorable brand identity becomes a key differentiator for success. Branding goes beyond visual elements; it is about conveying a unique personality, voice, and values that resonate with your target audience. In this chapter, we delve deeper into the world of branding, exploring the key aspects that will help you establish a compelling brand for your B2B SaaS startup.

1. Brand Statement - Defining Your Purpose, Vision, and Values

A powerful brand statement is the essence of your B2B SaaS startup's identity. It is the heart and soul of your branding efforts, defining your purpose, vision, and values. Your brand statement communicates the 'why' behind your business, answering fundamental questions like why you exist, what you aim to achieve, and the principles that guide your actions.

To craft an impactful brand statement, introspect deeply into your startup's core identity. Understand the pain points your product addresses, the aspirations it fulfills, and the impact it aims to make. A well-crafted brand statement should resonate with your target audience, create an emotional connection, and leave a lasting impression.

2. Packaging and Positioning - Presenting Your Unique Value Proposition

Packaging and positioning are two sides of the same branding coin. Packaging involves the visual representation of your B2B SaaS product, including the logo, design elements, and user interface. It is about creating an attractive and memorable visual identity that captures the essence of your brand. The packaging should reflect your brand personality, evoke the right emotions, and leave a positive impact on users.

Positioning, on the other hand, focuses on defining your unique value proposition. It answers the question of how your B2B SaaS solution is different from competitors and why customers should choose you. Effective positioning highlights the benefits users can expect from your product, aligning it with the specific needs and pain points of your target audience.

3. Workspace Experience & Management Style - Internal Branding

While external branding is crucial for engaging customers, internal branding is equally important for building a cohesive and aligned organizational culture. Your workspace experience and management style contribute to the overall branding by shaping the perception of employees, stakeholders, and partners.

A positive workspace experience fosters a sense of belonging, purpose, and well-being among employees. When your team feels connected to the brand's vision and values, it reflects in their work, interactions, and commitment to excellence. Similarly, a well-defined management style that aligns with your brand values helps maintain consistency in decision-making and actions, reinforcing your brand identity.

4. Pricing and Focus on Target Group - Brand Perception and Positioning

Pricing strategy is a strategic element of branding that significantly impacts brand perception and positioning. Your pricing decisions should align with your brand values and the expectations of your target audience. Whether you position your product as a premium offering or a budget-friendly solution, the pricing should reinforce your brand identity and communicate your product's value.

Understanding your target group is pivotal in shaping your branding efforts. Dive deep into their preferences, pain points, behavior, and aspirations. Tailor your messaging, communication, and marketing efforts to resonate with your ideal customers, creating a strong emotional connection that transcends transactional interactions.

5. Customer Support & Redressal - Reinforcing Brand Trust

Exceptional customer support is a cornerstone of successful branding for any B2B SaaS startup. When customers receive prompt, efficient, and personalized assistance, it not only resolves issues but also reinforces brand trust and loyalty. Your customer support experience is a reflection of your brand's commitment to customer satisfaction and portrays your startup as reliable, trustworthy, and customer-centric.

Implementing effective redressal mechanisms and actively seeking feedback from customers not only enhances your product but also provides valuable insights for further branding improvements. A responsive and empathetic approach to customer support reinforces your brand's human touch and demonstrates that you genuinely care about your customers' success.

Branding is not just about logos and colors; it is about creating a holistic and memorable identity that resonates with your target audience. By focusing on branding, you can differentiate your B2B SaaS startup, establish a unique personality, and build a loyal customer base that embraces your vision and values. Remember that branding is an ongoing process that requires consistency, innovation, and a deep understanding of your target audience's needs and aspirations. Embrace the power of branding to elevate your startup's success, leave a lasting impact on the world of B2B SaaS, and build a legacy that stands the test of time.

SEVENTEEN

DEVELOPING COMPELLING CONTENT AND CREATIVES

As you inch closer to the launch of your B2B SaaS startup, the focus now shifts to creating compelling content and creatives that will captivate your target audience and drive engagement. Content plays a pivotal role in establishing brand authority, educating potential customers, and driving conversions. In this chapter, we will explore the key elements of content development and how it ties into the PR strategy, marketing channels, and branding aspects discussed in previous chapters.

Understanding the Role of Content in Your Go To Market Strategy:

Content is the backbone of your Go To Market strategy. It acts as a bridge between your startup and your target audience, helping you connect, educate, and persuade potential customers to choose your business offering. As you develop content and creatives, keep in mind the insights gained from your PR strategy, marketing channel analysis, and branding convention.

1. Create a Captivating Landing Page:

Your landing page is the first touchpoint for your potential customers, and it should leave a lasting impression. Craft a landing page that is specific, minimal, and compelling. Use concise and persuasive content to highlight your product's features, explain how it works, provide access to technical documentation, and present clear pricing information. Include a contact form as a call-to-action to encourage sign-ups.

Case Study:

Company: XYZ Tech Solutions

Objective: To generate leads and sign-ups for a beta launch of a project management SaaS platform.

Landing Page Content:

Concise description of the project management platform, highlighting its key features and benefits.

Infographic showcasing the three-step process of how the platform streamlines project workflows.

Testimonials from beta users praising the platform's ease of use and efficiency.

Call-to-action button leading to a contact form for users to sign up for the beta launch.

2. Design Infographics for Visual Appeal:

Infographics are powerful tools for conveying complex information in a visually appealing manner. Design a three-step or five-step infographic that showcases what customers can achieve with your business offering. Ensure the value proposition is compelling and presented in an engaging design that captures attention.

3. Prepare Resource Materials:

Resource materials such as whitepapers, blogs, and ebooks play a crucial role in establishing your startup as an industry expert. These materials should provide valuable insights and practical solutions to the pain points of your target audience. Showcase your expertise, thought leadership, and domain knowledge to build trust and credibility.

Sample Case Study:

Company: ABC Marketing Solutions

Objective: To position the company as a thought leader in digital marketing and generate leads for their marketing automation SaaS platform.

Resource Material: EBook

Title: "Mastering Digital Marketing: A Comprehensive Guide for B2B Marketers"

Content:

Introduction to the challenges faced by B2B marketers in the digital landscape.

In-depth chapters on various digital marketing strategies, including SEO, content marketing, social media, and email marketing.

Case studies showcasing successful B2B marketing campaigns.

Practical tips and best practices for leveraging marketing automation tools.

4. Develop Email Drafts, Sales Templates & Phone-Calling Scripts:

As part of your Go To Market strategy, you need to equip your sales and marketing teams with effective communication tools. Develop email drafts, sales templates, and phone-calling scripts that are aligned with your branding guidelines and messaging. Ensure that these materials address the specific needs and pain points of your potential customers.

Sample Email Draft:

Subject: Enhance Your Project Management Efficiency with XYZ Tech Solutions

Dear [Name],

We hope this email finds you well. At XYZ Tech Solutions, we are excited to introduce our innovative project management SaaS platform, designed to streamline your project workflows and enhance team collaboration.

Our platform offers a user-friendly interface that simplifies project planning, task assignment, and progress tracking. With advanced features such as real-time updates, Gantt chart visualization, and resource allocation, you can ensure efficient project execution and timely deliveries.

We are currently offering an exclusive beta launch for select users, and we believe your team could benefit significantly from our platform. As a beta user, you will have the opportunity to provide valuable feedback and shape the future of our product.

To join our beta program, simply click on the link below to sign up. We look forward to having you onboard and revolutionizing the way your team manages projects.

[CTA Button: Sign Up Now]

Should you have any questions or require further information, feel free to reach out to our team at [Contact Number] or [Email Address]. We are here to assist you every step of the way.

Thank you for considering XYZ Tech Solutions. We are eager to partner with you in your journey to project management excellence.

Best regards,

[Signature]

Developing compelling content and creatives is an integral part of your Go To Market strategy for your B2B SaaS startup. It is the glue that holds your PR efforts, marketing channels, and branding together, forming a cohesive and powerful narrative. By creating captivating landing pages, infographics, and resource materials, you can educate and engage your target audience effectively. Integrating your content with your PR strategy and marketing channels ensures maximum visibility and impact. Moreover, consistent content development strengthens your branding, fostering trust and recognition among potential customers. Remember, the launch version and online courseware provide comprehensive insights and tools to help you craft persuasive content and creatives for a successful launch and beyond.

EIGHTEEN

TARGET - PITCH - RETARGET

As your B2B SaaS startup approaches its launch date, it's crucial to have a well-structured marketing strategy that effectively targets potential customers, delivers compelling pitches, and implements retargeting techniques to maximize conversions.

In this chapter, we will delve into the core aspects of marketing operations that revolve around reaching your target audience online, pitching your business offering to them, leveraging retargeting, and understanding the vital role of Conversion Rate Optimization (CRO).

1. Targeting Your Prospects:

Targeting your prospects is the foundation of successful digital advertising. This involves some basic setup of elements to capture, track, and process data. While the SOPs are available for delivery to your email, lets further dig deeper of the science behind this!

By identifying and reaching out to the right audience, you increase the chances of engagement and conversion.

Understanding your target audience's demographics, interests, and behavior is essential for precision targeting.

Utilizing Data-Driven Targeting:

Leverage data from your website analytics, social media insights, and customer databases to gain valuable insights into your audience's preferences and behaviors.

Utilize keyword research tools and audience segmentation to create targeted campaigns based on search patterns, interests, and demographics.

Case Study:

Company: XYZ Analytics Solutions

Objective: To target businesses looking for data analytics solutions in the retail industry.

Targeting Strategy:

Utilizing keyword planner to identify relevant keywords such as "retail data analytics," "business intelligence for retail," etc.

Narrowing the audience based on region and industry to focus on retail businesses seeking analytics solutions.

Implementing audience segmentation to target decision makers and data analysts in the retail sector.

2. Crafting Compelling Pitches:

Effective pitching is about delivering a persuasive and tailored message that resonates with your target audience. Whether it's through content marketing, social media, or email outreach, your pitch should clearly communicate the value proposition of your business offering and address your audience's pain points.

Creating Personalized Pitches:

Segment your audience and tailor your pitches to address specific pain points and challenges faced by each segment.

Craft compelling content that showcases how your SaaS solution can solve their unique problems and improve their business processes.

Sample Pitch:

Subject: Revolutionize Your Retail Business with Advanced Data Analytics

Dear [Recipient's Name],

Are you struggling to gain actionable insights from the vast amounts of data your retail business generates every day? XYZ Analytics Solutions is here to transform your data into a strategic asset.

Our advanced data analytics platform is specifically designed for retail businesses like yours. With real-time data visualization, predictive analytics, and AI-driven insights, you can make data-driven decisions that boost sales, optimize inventory, and enhance customer experiences.

Schedule a personalized demo today, and see how our analytics platform can revolutionize your retail business. Take the first step towards data-driven success!

Best regards,

[Signature]

3. Implementing Retargeting Techniques:

Retargeting, also known as remarketing, is a powerful strategy to stay connected with potential customers who have already visited your landing page or interacted with your website. By using cookies and data tracking, you can retarget these prospects with personalized ads, reminding them of your business offering and encouraging them to return.

The Power of Retargeting:

Implement retargeting pixels on your landing page to track visitor behavior and engagement.

Craft retargeting ads that are relevant and tailored to the specific actions taken by each prospect on your website.

Use retargeting to bring back bounced visitors, abandoned cart users, and potential customers who showed initial interest but didn't convert.

Case Study:

Company: ABC Cloud Services

Objective: To retarget potential customers who visited the website but didn't sign up for a free trial.

Retargeting Strategy:

Place retargeting pixels on the free trial sign-up page and specific product pages.

Segment the retargeting audience based on the level of engagement and actions taken on the website.

Deliver personalized retargeting ads highlighting the benefits of the free trial and offering exclusive incentives to encourage sign-ups.

4. The Vital Role of Conversion Rate Optimization (CRO):

Conversion Rate Optimization (CRO) plays a crucial role in improving the performance of your marketing operations. It focuses on maximizing the number of website visitors who take a desired action, such as signing up for a free trial or subscribing to your newsletter.

Key Elements of CRO:

A/B Testing: Conduct split tests to compare different versions of your landing page, emails, or ads to determine which performs better in terms of conversion rate.

Landing Page Optimization: Ensure that your landing page is user-friendly, loads quickly, and features clear and compelling calls-to-action.

Data Analysis: Regularly analyze website data to identify patterns, user behavior, and areas that need improvement for better conversion rates.

User Experience (UX) Design: Improve the overall user experience on your website to reduce bounce rates and increase engagement.

Case Study:

Company: Tech Solutions Inc.

Objective: To optimize the website's free trial sign-up page and increase the conversion rate.

CRO Strategy:

Conducted A/B testing for different variations of the sign-up page, including headline, CTA button, and form fields.

Implemented UX improvements to streamline the sign-up process and reduce friction.

Analyzed user behavior through heatmaps and data tracking to identify drop-off points and make necessary adjustments.

Mastering marketing operations for your B2B SaaS startup requires a well-planned approach to target your prospects, craft compelling pitches, implement effective retargeting techniques, and optimize your conversion rates through CRO. By leveraging data-driven targeting, creating personalized pitches, and implementing retargeting strategies, you can maximize engagement and conversions. Remember, successful marketing operations require constant analysis, optimization, and alignment with your overall Go To Market strategy. Stay agile, adapt to market changes, and continuously refine your marketing operations to achieve sustainable growth and success for your startup.

NINETEEN

CREATING A NURTURE STREAM

In the realm of B2B SaaS marketing, lead nurturing is a critical component of the customer acquisition process. Nurture streams are automated workflows that trigger actions based on a prospect's behavior in response to your marketing efforts. This chapter delves into the creation of a nurture stream, using a whitepaper as a lead magnet, to engage and convert prospects effectively.

1. Leveraging Whitepapers as Lead Magnets:

Having personally seen great results with EdTech, and Energy & Power SaaS startups, I'd often vouch for writing such resource materials. Whitepapers are highly valuable and informative technical documents that attract industry leaders and prospects seeking in-depth insights. As gated content, visitors are required to provide their name and email address to access these documents, making them ideal lead magnets.

Creating a Compelling Whitepaper:

Focus on a specific pain point or industry challenge that your target audience faces.

Offer data-driven research, case studies, and actionable solutions in the whitepaper.

Include a clear call-to-action (CTA) encouraging prospects to sign up for further communications.

2. Designing a Sample Nurture Stream:

Let me brief this case with my favorite activity! A nurture stream for a whitepaper can be automated to engage prospects who have downloaded the document and those who haven't. The workflow can be designed as follows:

Scenario 1: Prospects Who Downloaded the Whitepaper

Day 1: Send a thank-you email with additional resources and related content.

Day 5: Share a customer success story or testimonial related to the whitepaper's topic.

Day 10: Offer a free webinar or demo related to the whitepaper's insights.

Webinar Landing Page: Create a dedicated landing page for the webinar with a clear CTA to register.

Email Invitation: Send personalized email invitations to prospects who downloaded the whitepaper, inviting them to the webinar.

Webinar Reminder Emails: Send multiple reminders leading up to the webinar date, with exciting teasers about the content.

Day 15: Send a personalized follow-up email, inviting them to schedule a consultation.

Post-Webinar Follow-Up: Send a follow-up email to webinar attendees, thanking them for their participation, and offering additional resources based on the webinar's content.

Day 20: Share a case study that highlights the success of a client who applied the whitepaper's strategies.

Day 25: Send a survey to gather feedback and understand their pain points better.

Day 30: Offer an exclusive discount or limited-time promotion for your product or service.

Scenario 2: Prospects Who Haven't Downloaded the Whitepaper

Day 3: Send a reminder email highlighting the value and benefits of the whitepaper.

Day 7: Share an infographic or key statistics from the whitepaper to pique interest.

Day 12: Offer a limited-time promotion or discount related to the whitepaper's topic.

Day 18: Send a final reminder email, emphasizing the time-sensitive nature of the offer.

Day 23: Share a video testimonial from a satisfied client who benefited from the whitepaper.

Day 28: Offer a personalized consultation with your team to discuss their pain points.

Day 33: Send a follow-up email with relevant blog posts or articles related to the whitepaper's topic.

3. Integrating Nurture Stream with Go To Market Strategy:

In the context of Go To Market strategy, nurture streams play a crucial role in automating premeditated tasks for launch events, such as webinars. The nurture stream can include multiple reminders to drive registrations and attendance, followed by post-event follow-ups.

Automating the Webinar Process:

Pre-Event: Send multiple email reminders to prospects encouraging them to register.

Webinar Registration Confirmation: Send an automated email confirming their registration and providing them with the webinar details and link to add to their calendar.

During Event: Automate reminders to attendees to increase engagement during the webinar.

Webinar Reminder Emails: Send automated reminders a day before, an hour before, and 10 minutes before the webinar to maximize attendance.

Post-Event: Send thank-you emails to attendees and follow-up emails to those who missed it.

Webinar Follow-Up: Send a follow-up email to attendees, thanking them for their participation, and offering additional resources based on the webinar's content.

Post-Event (Continued): Share a recording of the webinar and additional resources for attendees.

Webinar Recording and Resources: Send automated follow-up emails to both attendees and no-shows, providing them with a link to access the webinar recording and additional resources.

4. Utilizing Data Points for Effective Nurture Stream:

Nurture streams are based on simple data points like email opens, clicks, registrations, and attendance. However, the depth and complexity of the nurture stream can be enhanced through Conversion Rate Optimization (CRO) data and user tracking.

Using Conversion Rate Optimization (CRO) Insights:

Heatmaps: Analyze data from heatmaps and user tracking to identify areas for improvement, like CTA button placement and content engagement.

Dwell Time and Engagement: Measure the time prospects spend on specific sections of your landing pages, providing insights into their interests and pain points.

5. Compliance Aspects of Sending Marketing Communications:

Compliance is crucial when sending marketing communications. It's essential to obtain explicit consent from prospects before sending any promotional emails or communications.

Ensure Compliance with GDPR and CAN-SPAM Laws:

Consent: Prospects must opt-in to receive marketing communications and be informed about the purpose of collecting their data.

Unsubscribe Option: Include an easy-to-find unsubscribe option in every marketing email, giving recipients the choice to opt-out at any time.

Creating a nurture stream is a powerful tool in lead nurturing and customer acquisition for B2B SaaS startups. By leveraging whitepapers as lead magnets, designing sample nurture streams, and integrating them with your Go To Market strategy, you can effectively engage and convert prospects. Utilize data points and CRO insights to refine your nurture stream, ensuring it aligns with your overall marketing objectives. Embrace automation, personalize your communication, and stay agile in adapting your nurture stream to the evolving needs of your prospects, ultimately driving sustainable growth and success for your startup. Comply with GDPR and CAN-SPAM laws to maintain ethical marketing practices and build a trustworthy brand.

TWENTY

LAUNCH DAY ACTIVITIES

The launch day of your B2B SaaS product is a culmination of weeks, if not months, of planning, strategizing, and hard work. It's the day you introduce your business offering to the world, and it's crucial to make it a memorable and impactful event.

In this chapter, we will delve deeper into the key activities and strategies to ensure a successful and flawless product launch.

1. Visualizing the Launch Day:

As the big day approaches, take some time to visualize how you want the launch to unfold. What impression do you want to leave on your audience?

Are you planning to deliver a product demo that wows them? Or do you want to showcase the unique features and benefits of your offering through a compelling sales deck?

Maybe you envision delivering an inspiring CEO address that resonates with your target audience.

Prepare a script or outline for your chosen approach to ensure a smooth and engaging presentation.

2. Engaging the Media:

Launching your product doesn't just mean holding a traditional press meet. In today's digital world, media refers to various communication platforms that can help you reach your target audience effectively. Consider using a webinar platform to present your product to a wider audience or create a pre-recorded video that can be shared across different channels.

Webinar Platform:

Choose a reliable and user-friendly webinar platform that can accommodate your audience size.

Test the platform beforehand to ensure a seamless experience during the event.

Prepare detailed instructions for participants, such as how to ask questions or access support.

3. The Power of Detailing:

Before your scheduled session begins, ensure you address all the intricacies to deliver a flawless presentation. Whether it's a live webinar or an offline event, paying attention to detail is essential for a successful launch.

Webinar Example:

11:00 AM: Start the event with a warm greeting and a quick sound check, asking participants to indicate if they can hear you.

11:03 AM: Proceed with the actual introduction, and allow a few more minutes for latecomers to join.

During the Presentation: Clearly instruct participants on how to reach the presenter, participate in Q&A, or seek internal support.

4. Leveraging Online Events:

Online events, such as webinars, offer unique advantages for product launches. These platforms allow you to interact with your audience in real-time, creating a sense of engagement and personalization. Additionally, webinars can be recorded and shared later for those who couldn't attend live.

Offline Events:

If you're hosting an offline event, prepare a compelling PowerPoint presentation to engage your audience visually.

Practice your speech and anticipate potential questions or challenges that may arise during the event.

5. Comprehensive Walkthrough in the Launch Version:

The launch version of your product should include a comprehensive walkthrough of all launch day activities. Provide detailed guidelines on recommended platforms, dos and don'ts for presentations, and use-cases beyond webinars. Cover the different aspects of online and offline events to ensure your team is well-prepared for any scenario.

6. Effective Communication Channels:

Choosing the right communication channels is crucial for promoting your launch and engaging your target audience effectively.

Social Media:

Utilize various social media platforms to generate buzz and excitement around the launch.

Share teasers and sneak peeks of your product to build anticipation among your audience.

Create engaging visuals, videos, and infographics to capture attention and increase reach.

Email Marketing:

Send personalized email invitations to key stakeholders and target customers.

Include a clear call-to-action and a link to the launch event registration or access page.

Follow up with reminder emails to ensure maximum attendance and excitement.

7. Dos and Don'ts for the Launch:

To ensure a successful launch, keep the following dos and don'ts in mind:

Dos:

Plan Ahead: Plan and rehearse your launch activities well in advance to avoid last-minute issues.

Engage Your Audience: Interact with your audience during the event, addressing their questions and concerns to create a sense of connection.

Provide Value: Focus on delivering value to your audience through insightful content and engaging presentations.

Don'ts:

Overwhelm Your Audience: Keep your presentation concise and avoid overwhelming your audience with too much information.

Neglect Preparation: Thoroughly prepare for the launch to avoid any technical glitches or unanticipated challenges.

Forget to Follow Up: After the launch, follow up with attendees, thanking them for their participation and providing additional resources or offers.

8. Drip Nurture Campaign Setup and Communication Channels:

Incorporate drip nurture campaigns into your launch strategy. A drip nurture campaign is a sequence of pre-scheduled, automated emails that are sent to prospects at specific intervals. Today, we have integrated SMS & WhatsApp triggers in addition to email communications may be used effectively as well.

This helps keep your audience engaged even after the launch and can drive them towards conversion.

Communication Channels:

Use email marketing to send out drip nurture campaigns.

Consider personalized follow-up emails to specific segments of your audience based on their interactions with your product.

9. Compliance with Data Protection Laws:

Compliance with data protection laws, such as GDPR, is vital while handling customer data for launch communication. Ensure that you obtain explicit consent from recipients to receive marketing communications, and provide easy options for them to unsubscribe from your email list.

The product launch day is a momentous occasion for any B2B SaaS startup. By visualizing the day's events, leveraging media platforms, paying attention to detailing, and utilizing effective communication channels, you can ensure a successful and impactful launch. Embrace the power of online events, such as webinars, and make use of comprehensive walkthroughs and guidelines to navigate through the launch process seamlessly. Remember to comply with data protection laws and engage your audience with valuable and engaging content, ultimately setting the stage for a successful and fruitful product launch.

TWENTY-ONE

LEAD GENERATION, CONVERSIONS, AND STREAMLINING BUSINESS OPERATIONS

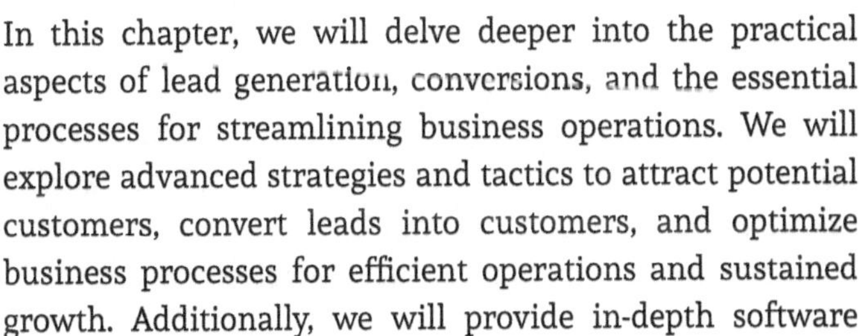

In this chapter, we will delve deeper into the practical aspects of lead generation, conversions, and the essential processes for streamlining business operations. We will explore advanced strategies and tactics to attract potential customers, convert leads into customers, and optimize business processes for efficient operations and sustained growth. Additionally, we will provide in-depth software suggestions and detailed process flow samples as case studies to illustrate effective implementation.

1. Advanced Lead Generation Strategies:

Effective lead generation requires a combination of traditional and cutting-edge strategies. Let's explore some advanced lead generation tactics:

Software Suggestions:

LeadFeeder: Identify website visitors and potential leads based on their interaction with your website, helping you target interested prospects.

LinkedIn Sales Navigator: Leverage the power of LinkedIn to find and engage with potential customers based on specific criteria such as industry, job title, and company size.

Web Personalization Tools: Utilize web personalization tools to customize website content based on visitor behavior and preferences, providing a personalized experience.

Process Flow Sample - Advanced Lead Generation:

Implement LeadFeeder to identify potential leads visiting your website and gather valuable information about their behavior and interests.

Utilize LinkedIn Sales Navigator to connect with decision-makers and key stakeholders in target industries, initiating personalized conversations.

Utilize web personalization tools to display customized content and offers to website visitors based on their past interactions and interests.

Implement exit-intent pop-ups to capture leads who are about to leave your website without taking action, encouraging them to stay engaged.

2. Advanced Lead Conversion Strategies:

Converting leads into customers requires a strategic approach and personalized engagement. Let's explore advanced lead conversion strategies:

Software Suggestions:

Intercom: Engage with website visitors in real-time through live chat, targeted messages, and personalized support.

User Onboarding Tools: Use user onboarding tools to guide new leads through the sign-up process and demonstrate the value of your offering.

Automated Email Sequences: Set up automated email sequences using tools like ActiveCampaign or Drip to nurture leads and move them through the sales funnel.

Process Flow Sample - Advanced Lead Conversion:

Utilize Intercom to engage with website visitors in real-time, addressing their queries and providing personalized assistance.

Implement user onboarding tools to guide new leads through the sign-up process and showcase the key features and benefits of your product.

Create automated email sequences tailored to different segments of leads, delivering relevant content and offers to nurture them towards conversion.

Utilize behavioral tracking and analytics to identify high-intent leads and trigger personalized follow-up communications.

3. Optimizing Business Operations for Efficiency:

Streamlining business operations involves optimizing workflows, automating repetitive tasks, and enhancing collaboration among team members.

Furthermore, this will also help your organization pass certain data security, systems and process management compliances.

Software Suggestions:

Zapier: Connect and automate processes between different apps and tools, reducing manual work and streamlining workflows.

Trello: Use Trello boards to visually manage projects and tasks, assign responsibilities, and track progress.

Customer Success Platforms: Implement customer success platforms like Gainsight or Totango to proactively manage customer relationships and identify upsell opportunities.

Process Flow Sample - Optimizing Business Operations:

Integrate various apps and tools using Zapier to automate data transfer and streamline workflows across different departments.

Utilize Trello boards to visualize project progress, assign tasks, and ensure effective communication and collaboration within the team.

Implement customer success platforms to track customer interactions, identify potential issues, and proactively engage with customers to ensure their success.

Conduct regular team meetings and performance reviews to identify bottlenecks, optimize processes, and foster a culture of continuous improvement.

By adopting advanced lead generation and conversion strategies, and optimizing business operations through the implementation of cutting-edge tools and tactics, you can gain a competitive edge and position your business for long-term success. Remember that successful lead generation and conversions require a deep understanding of your target audience and a commitment to providing value at every touchpoint. By continuously refining your marketing efforts, optimizing business processes, and fostering a customer-centric culture, you can build a thriving and sustainable business in today's dynamic marketplace. Stay agile, embrace innovation, and never stop learning and adapting to the ever-evolving landscape of business and technology.

Lastword

We set deadlines to work on something great. We aim to meet them in a diligent and relaxed fashion. But then, we all tend to slow down at some point. We often start well but get a little sluggish as we progress, and at one point, we begin to procrastinate!

Tim Urban, a popular writer and a TED speaker, beautifully narrated the kind of approach people take to achieve a certain goal: "Our brain has three characters – a rational decision-maker, an instant gratification monkey, and a panic monster. The rational decision-maker is a great planner and is known to draft solid plans to achieve the set goal. However, the instant gratification monkey would just mislead you into wasting all the planned time by diverting your focus into something unnecessary. And, there is yet another character, the panic monster, who is the only person the monkey is afraid of. The panic monster would be idle for most of the time and would surface only when you are close to the deadline to meet your goals. The panic monster would help the rational decision-maker to take control of the situation before it's too late."

"This book is for innovators and startups who have experienced the wrath of this panic monster in the past. I have personally faced situations when I had to meet a deadline. The instant gratification monkey would deviate me from doing the work. Sometimes, I would completely go blank when the panic monster kicks in, so much that even the rational decision-maker in me went clueless as well."

"Honestly, I am not a great planner. In my opinion, planning involves breaking down a lot of tasks that would, in general, show how humongous time, energy, and effort are required. Planning would end up overwhelming."

"Let's admit it. Our attention spans are low, and we all love to see quick results, and on the other hand, we would want a great outcome too. Isn't it an oxymoron? There should be a way out of this mental trap, right? The Three Week Theory is designed to strike a balance with seemingly achievable tasks to do within a relatively shorter timeframe."

"Right after college, I started as an entrepreneur. I wish I knew all the critical aspects of starting up that I know now, back then! We, the startups, even as we learn to develop Go To Market strategy at the early stage, may face challenges to afford all the required resources. At times, we have to take it up all by ourselves. Bootstrappers often feel the stress of acquiring early customers and/or investments."

"Salesqualifyd is written, keeping in mind the mindset of startups. Having seen several startups succeed (and several fail), I have been trying to decode what makes a startup successful. It is often observed that big things are fashioned by small things done well."

"A successful Go To Market strategy is all about ensuring that nothing is ignored, i.e., ensuring the 'small things' are taken care of. Apparently, as startups, we tend not to prioritize such 'small things,' which would eventually give us headaches when we are close to a deadline."

"This book is not a guide to Go To Market. It is written based on my observations on how these 'small things' sabotaged 'big plans' and to show those 'small things' their place by keeping a tab on them.

A startup might have got an idea, maybe after facing a treacherous experience in certain cases, and would persistently pursue it for months together! Salesqualifyd is a 21-day taskmaster for innovators to sit back and set a framework on how they would be getting ready for their launch."

"One day at a time. One aspect every day to ensure a fail-safe approach to Go To Market."

"Why this 'Three Week Theory'? It rhymed and sounded well! I'm a great fan of Harsha Bhogle. In 2009, the organizers of the Indian Premier League had to make a crucial call due to assembly elections. With only three weeks to go, they had one decision to make! They chose to go ahead with the scheduled itinerary by moving the entire tournament to South Africa. He said, '...we did it, you know why? Because no country in the world works as slow as we do until the last three weeks before an event, and no country in the world works as fast as we do in the last three weeks before an event,' and the statement holds correct. Right from organizing professional events to weddings at home, substantial progress happens only in the last three weeks. Going To Market is a landmark event for innovators! Make it a successful, memorable, and scalable one."

"I trust this concept would make sense to you."

"Happy Hustling!"

Balaji Vijayaraghavan